When Life is Hard

When Life is Hard

50 Reminders that God is Near

Stacy Averette, Ed.D.

ISBN-13: 9798573505978

To Eric

Thank you for believing in this book before I did

Contents

Acknowledgments

My life has been abundantly blessed by countless people who have invested in me. I am especially grateful for the friends who have been by my side in life, ministry, and business, through the hard times and the celebrations. There are too many to name, but you know who you are.

I am especially grateful to Rob, Ann, Lucille, Sara, and Camilla for your friendship and assistance.

To my dear friend and mentor, Dr. Robert Mathis: Your encouragement made all the difference. I still hear your voice cheering me on.

To my parents, J.C. and Faye Smitherman, and my grandparents, Doris and Lester Owens: Your impact on my life is immeasurable. I'm blessed by your legacy and I miss each of you every day.

To Eric, Jon and Molly, Maddie and John, and Caleb: You are my dearest friends. I thank you for your love and patience and the joy and laughter you have given me over the years. I love you all.

Preface

One of my fears is that what I refer to as "hard times" in this book won't seem hard to you at all. No doubt you've been through (or are going through) much harder times than what I've written about here. So have I. But I don't feel called to share those.

The stories I share are to remind you how very much God cares for you even on your ordinary days when life is hard. Sometimes "hard" is simply the last, small straw that *breaks the camel's back*. I think we tend to downplay God's nearness during those times. We don't have to white-knuckle our way through or put on our big girl pants and deal with it alone.

Jesus helped out a hostess at a wedding reception and fed some hungry people on a hillside. He cared that a few fishermen were discouraged by their empty nets and he took notice of a guy in a tree watching from a distance. We highlight His big miracles and sometimes miss that the biggest miracle of all is that He sees, cares, and acts on our behalf on our ordinary days.

God cares about you and will show Himself near to you in a thousand little ways during every season of life. That's what I want you to take away from this book. When you finish the last page I hope my stories, my testimony, will help you know Him better and love Him more.

I will lift up my eyes to the hills.
From where does my help come?
My help comes from the LORD,
who made heaven and earth.

He will not let your foot be moved;
he who keeps you will not slumber.
Behold, he who keeps Israel
will neither slumber nor sleep.

The LORD is your keeper;
the LORD is your shade on your right hand.
The sun shall not strike you by day,
nor the moon by night.

The LORD will keep you from all evil;
he will keep your life.
The LORD will keep
your going out and your coming in
from this time forth and forevermore.
(Ps 121)

Introduction

"This isn't what I signed up for," I thought to myself halfway through the race. We'd trained well for the first 5k of the year but it was colder than predicted and the race course included a muddy road on the back side of a hay field. I left the trail to dodge the mess a few times and ended up in the thorn bushes hugging the fence row.

If I'd known all the facts ahead of time I might have made a different choice. Played it safe. Stayed home. But I would've missed so much.

Life is full of surprises, too. Hard times come and they don't look anything like what we thought they would. You know a thing a two about hard times don't you? And I'll bet you've developed some "hard-times-muscles" to help you get through? But still you wonder, "Am I the only one struggling?" or "What can I do to make it easier now and down the road?" Friend, I want you to know you're not the only one! Somehow knowing that makes it easier, doesn't it?

Life is hard. We live in a fallen world groaning for redemption and restoration.

What can you do to make life's struggles easier? You could read the latest self-help book or enroll in an online self-improvement course. You could commit to a new diet and exercise plan or learn how to manage your money and stick to a budget. You could get a degree and the job of your dreams. You could get rid of your current toxic relationships and find a new set of friends. And still, hard times would come because we live in a fallen world. Heaven is the eternal perfect home for all believers, but we're not there yet.

As for all the suggestions I made about making life easier, well, I've tried most of them and some might actually improve your life. But the only place I've found deeply satisfying, lasting hope is in God's Word. The Bible is a spiritual compass that points us to Jesus and reorients our life to walk in His steps.

> Therefore, since we are surrounded by so great a cloud of witnesses, let us lay aside every weight, and sin which clings so closely, and let us run with endurance the race that is set before us, looking to Jesus, the founder and perfecter of our faith, who for the joy that was set before him endured the cross, despising the shame, and is seated at the right hand of the throne of God. (Heb 12:1-2)

During the back country 5k my hope of finishing the race well was bolstered by the encouragers around me. My training partner and friend ran with me every step of the way. Throughout the race there were encouragers and cheerleaders who knew the route, pointing us in the right direction. They clapped and chanted and cheered us on at every obstacle until we reached the finish line.

If you're weary in your race today I'm cheering you on, reminding you that the finish line is just ahead and that as a child of God, you do not run alone.

The book you hold is a compilation of stories. Each chapter stands on its own as a testimony of God's faithfulness on a hard day or during a hard season. You may choose to read it cover to cover, but feel free to skip around and read what speaks to you each day. Each chapter ends with a "Takeaway Truth" straight from God's Word. My words and advice may be flawed and biased and unhelpful. God's Word is perfect in every way for every person in every season.

I have found God to be sufficient in the midst of all my troubles. I pray this book reminds and encourages you to rest in Him.

1

When Hard Times Come

When hard times come, trust God. Lean into Him. Call out to Him. Cry out to Him.

I know for sure you can do this without speaking a word. He hears the groaning of your heart.

We sing lyrics that say "lean on me when you're not strong". Lean on whom? All flesh and blood are weary from hard times. Burdens are heavy. We each have our own and hesitate to add to a friend's burden by sharing ours. Sometimes we blurt it out hoping the release will bring relief. But not all are equipped and ready to listen and be leaned on. The disregard and disconnection we encounter from other weary travelers only hurts us more.

The Liar will blame someone, anyone, and invite you to a party thrown by Pity. Hopelessness is his theme. "Give up and give in," he whispers. "This is as good as it gets."

Decline his offer. Ignore his lies. There's a better way to deal. Learn to lean on Jesus.

Life *is* hard. But He is strong and able to carry us through. He's taken on the sin of the world and won. Daily He invites us to celebrate the Eternal Hope we have in Him!

Takeaway Truth

"Who shall separate us from the love of Christ? Shall tribulation, or distress, or persecution, or famine, or nakedness, or danger, or sword? As it is written, 'For your sake we are being killed all the day long; we are regarded as sheep to be slaughtered.' No, in all these things we are more than conquerors through him who loved us." (Rom 8:35-37)

2

When You're Tired of Being Strong

Do not pray for an easier life, pray to be a stronger person.

A poster with that anonymous quote hung in my kitchen 20 years ago. I was a young wife and mother of three, working full-time, trying to be a strong person but secretly wishing for an easier life. I was tired of being strong

Fast forward to today. I'm a fifty-something wife and mother in a different season trying to be a strong person but, often, still wishing for an easier life---at least an easy day---every now and then.

Maybe I don't even want easy. How about just not so hard? On the "so hard" days grief, difficult relationships, heartbreak, and "how will we pay for that?" collide to create the perfect storm.

A recent Saturday was one of those days I was hoping for "easy". I mean, we expect Monday to be hard, right? But Saturday? Saturday wears comfy clothes and goes on bike rides and picnics in the sunshine with a perfect, cool breeze blowing. Saturday walks slower than Thursday and enjoys a second cup of coffee with Conversation and Big Dreams. Saturday catches her breath and counts her blessings as she watches the sunset.

Your Saturdays look like that, right? Yeah, mine either.

Well, not all of them do, but I try to be intentional about slowing down, setting aside the list, and savoring this one life. So we enjoy a late breakfast with our people eating waffles and drinking chocolate milk. There's menu planning, our weekly trip to Aldi, a little thrift therapy followed by a simple lunch, in the car, under a shade tree. All through the day we spoke this to one another:

"Humble yourselves, therefore, under the mighty hand of God so that at the proper time he may exalt you, casting all your anxieties on him, because he cares for you. Be sober-minded; be watchful. Your adversary the devil prowls around like a roaring lion, seeking someone to devour." (I Pet 5:6-8)

Saturday started out as a lovely day. She lived up to all my expectations of perfect Saturdays. Until she didn't. The dark clouds in the sky mirrored the ones in my heart and mind.

It's like that sometimes, right? A summer thunderstorm appears out of nowhere and threatens to wash away our best laid plans. We're suddenly drenched heavy, with raindrops and disappointment.

Then I remember the words from the Word laid out on my lap in the early morning; soul food that nourished before breakfast. The underlined verse and two words looked up and written down, break through the storm like a rainbow promise.

"The Lord is a refuge for the oppressed, a stronghold in times of trouble." (Ps 9:9 New International Version)

Refuge: condition of being safe or sheltered from pursuit, danger, or trouble

Stronghold: a place that has been fortified so as to protect it against attack.

Takeaway Truth

1. We will have trouble in this life. That's a guarantee according to Jesus. "I have said these things to you, that in me you may have peace. In the world you will have tribulation. But take heart; I have overcome the world." (John 16:33)

2. We can't always control the trouble. Try as we might to orchestrate easy days, some hit us hard. Are we only at the mercy of the trouble that comes our way? Not according to God's Word. Jesus is our very present help in times of trouble if we will but call out to Him in our need.

Sometimes He calms the storms around us. Sometimes He calms the storm within us.

3. We can control what and how we think in the trouble. Last year I spent two weeks in a third world country and I often feel guilty when I'm overwhelmed and in need of help. I hear my adversary mocking me and my "first world problems" and shaming my escape to the Refuge and Stronghold who's overcome it all. In

those moments I think about how much God loves me and wants to help me. He loves you and wants to help you, too. He is an ever present help in every kind of trouble.

"God is our refuge and strength, a very present help in trouble." (Ps 46:1)

4. We should stop praying to be a stronger person and pray to be strong in the Lord. It's a subtle, yet significant difference. Our flesh (pride) despises weakness but in weakness we find that only the strength of the Lord can make us strong. That's worth repeating. Only the strength of the Lord can make us strong.

As a Christ follower, down is the new up. Weak is the new strong. Humble is the new proud.

Jesus has overcome the world. He is our peace. He is our strength.

See here:

God is our refuge and strength. (Ps 46:1-3)

The name of the Lord is a strong tower. (Prov 18:10)

The joy of the Lord is your strength. (Neh 8:10)

The Lord is my strength. (Ex 15:2)

In God you have an everlasting rock. (Isa 26:3-4)

Seek the Lord and His strength. (I Chron 16:11)

The Lord is the stronghold of my life. (Ps 27:1-3)

3

When You're Weary of Serving Others

Why do you do what you do? Why do you do your job, volunteer projects, mission trips, cooking for your family, decorating your house, helping in Vacation Bible School? Is it because you feel you have to? Is it because you think no one else will do it if you don't? Is it because you think it will make you feel better? Is it because you think it will make someone else feel better? Is it because you think it's the right thing to do? You may be right. I know how you feel.

I also know that doing and serving for those reasons alone eventually causes me to feel bitter, unappreciated, taken-for-granted, and resentful. The unpleasant feelings that rear their ugly heads a thousand times a week are the reason why I keep this reminder on the bathroom door. I frequently need to be reminded.

"Even as the Son of Man came not to be served but to serve, and to give his life as a ransom for many." (Matt 20:28)

Oswald Chambers said:

> The mainspring of service is not love for man, but love for Jesus Christ. If we are devoted to the cause of humanity we shall soon be crushed and broken-hearted, for we shall often meet with more ingratitude from men than we would from a dog, but if our motive is love to God, no ingratitude can hinder us from serving our fellow man.

> When we realize that Jesus served us to the end of our meanness, our selfishness, our sin, nothing we meet with from others can exhaust our determination to serve men for His sake.[1]

The things you and I do must be done as if God Himself had asked us to. For me, that changes everything.

Takeaway Truth

"Whatever you do, work heartily, as for the Lord and not for men," (Col 3:23)

4

When You're on the Verge of a Breakdown

I love to travel. Well, sort of. I really like the thought of traveling more than the actual process of packing stuff and leaving home.

Hello. My name is Stacy and I'm a homebody. Staying home is my favorite. But a friend needed some help and my husband, Eric, said it would do me good. I said "yes" to the invitation and was a wee bit excited until the itinerary showed up in my inbox. I thought of my list and my calendar and what I'd miss. I thought of all that could go wrong. Was it was too late to change my mind? No, but yes.

My bags were packed along with a load of ambivalence. We said our goodbyes, hugged and kissed, and off I went trying to outrun the clouds.

The Breakdown

I was on the verge of a break down. Really. Like, my car with the new engine and the new tires and the new transmission and the new water pump was about to break down an hour from home. It went something like this.

Me: What's that's smell? Hmmm. Car's running fine. Gauges all read normal. Somebody in this traffic 'bout to break down. Probably that ol' truck over there.

(Drives a few more miles.)

Me: There's that smell again. I must be following that ol' truck that's 'bout to break down.

(Check gauges. Keep driving.)

Me: *Sniff. Sniff.* Again? Uh-Oh!

(Check gauges. Say some Christian cuss words in my head. Look for a gas station. Pull over. Turn off the engine. Grab my phone.)

Me: "Hey. I'm broke down." (Ain't nobody got time for good grammar when you break down.)

Husband: "Nooo! Where? What's wrong?"

I explain and send a photo of the puddle of liquid-something beneath my car. He diagnoses the problem, calls the mechanic, calls the wrecker, calls me back, and rearranges his schedule.

And I wait.

From the look of the beautiful blue sky you'd think I'd outrun the dark clouds of circumstance. Nope. Apparently not.

Me: Why is this happening to me? Maybe I shouldn't even be going on this trip. Why does this always happen to me? "Lord, what are you trying to teach me?" I asked out loud sitting in my car.

God: (silence)

My husband arrives and talks to the wrecker driver as he prepares to haul the car back to our mechanic. I jump in the car with my husband and he hauls me to my friend's house a few hours away.

As we leave the gas station I look up and see the giant sign: SMILE. SMILE Fuel is the name of the service station and I'd been parked in front of it all this time, sweating in the hot car, just wanting to go home, and asking God all my questions.

Jesus: "Now that's funny, don't you think?"

Me: "If you say so, Lord."

My friend and I made it to our tropical destination. The next morning I got up early to have my quiet time. The Old Testament Bible reading for the day was Habakkuk, a short book with just three chapters. When I open my Bible, the "Personal Application" in the introduction to the Scripture has these words underlined already: (Clearly, I've needed this lesson before.)

> Habakkuk reminds us that the question "Why?" can, should, and must be asked. Because he believed God, he believed that God had an answer to his problem. His questions demonstrated the presence of faith, not the lack of it.
>
> For an atheist, "Why?" has no meaning; for a believer, "Why?" finds its ultimate answer in God.

> The final verses of this prophecy teach that it is possible to rise above circumstances, and even to rejoice in them, by focusing on God who stands above all. Habakkuk does not deny his problems, nor does he treat them lightly; instead, he finds God sufficient in the midst of his troubles.[1]

Yeah. That.

I know there are worse problems than a busted heater hose. Really, I do. I've lived through worse and I'm wrestling something bigger even as I reflect on this break down. But that's the very point of it all for you and for me. God stands above it all. He is sufficient in the midst of all our troubles.

Are you on the verge of a break down? Overwhelmed by the circumstances of your life? Can I just encourage you to exercise your faith and ask God "Why?" and "What do you want to teach me, Lord?" He's right there in the middle of whatever you're going through "ready to show Himself strong on your behalf." (2 Chron 16:9) Invite Him in. Listen for His voice. Find answers in His Word.

Takeaway Truth

"But the righteous shall live by his faith." (Hab 2:4)

"For the earth will be filled with the knowledge of the glory of the Lord as the waters cover the sea." (Hab 2:14)

"Though the fig tree should not blossom, nor fruit be on the vines, the produce of the olive fail and the fields yield no food, the flock be cut off from the fold and there be no herd in the stalls, yet I will rejoice in the Lord; I will take joy in the God of my salvation." (Hab 3:17-18)

5

When You Want Your Life to Matter

Some time ago I was invited to speak at the Metairie Baptist Church Annual Women's Tea. I served as the Youth Minister there years ago when I was a seminary student. This seemed like the perfect time for a family get-away and a bit of a homecoming. We were thrilled to introduce our children to good food, good music, and the great friends we had in New Orleans.

The planning started with Terry. She was the Women's Ministry Coordinator at the time; she and her husband were youth parents back in our youth ministry days at MBC. When she invited all six of us to stay in her home while we were in New Orleans I couldn't have been more excited!

As a young woman I spent many, many hours in her home and those long, often late-night conversations were just one of the many ways I learned how to be a wife, mother, homemaker, and servant in the Body of Christ. Her home was always open (at least I thought it was) and I would drop by as often as possible, usually unannounced. She would welcome me with a smile and then continue with whatever she was doing before I arrived.

How Her Life Changed Mine

For years I had the privilege of watching her live out her ordinary days of cooking, cleaning, mothering, planning and serving. Her life changed mine. I am a better wife, mother, friend, and woman because of her example.

As we reconnected via email in the days leading up the event I shared with her what her friendship had meant to me. Once we arrived at her home prior to the event there were several more hours of late night conversations to catch up on the last two decades. We talked and laughed with my children gathered around (hers are all grown now) and I was reminded all over again about the ripple effect of our life. Who my children are today is due in part to the investment she made in my life years ago, and I am so thankful. I don't have enough words to express my gratitude to her (and many others) for the investment they've made in my life but I'll never stop trying to pay it forward.

I'm Not All That (but I'd like to be)

A few days after our family returned home from our trip to New Orleans, I shared about Terry and the event on my blog. Terry replied to me via email and said, "Wow! I'm really not all that! But I do love the fact that you think I am!"

If I'd written about you, you may have responded the same way. Most of us don't see ourselves as "great". We're pretty certain that our names will never be found in a history book and we're okay with that. But we all long to know that our lives have mattered in some way. Significance is a longing placed in every human heart by our Creator. The trouble comes in the ways we try to achieve greatness and significance.

Terry went on in her email to tell me the story of Aunt Emma Lou, her favorite aunt. Since I've never met her, she tried to describe what her Aunt meant to so many. As she wrote, I read simple stories of Aunt Emma Lou just being Aunt Emma Lou; but nothing that will make the history books. Then I read these words, "Her love and godly example had such an impact on me".

Aunt Emma Lou's life ripples through eternity. The way she lived changed Terry's life and in turn changed mine.

Aunt Emma Lou is dying and Terry is grieving the few short days she has left with her. I'll not have the privilege of thanking Aunt Emma Lou in this life for how she changed mine. But I did the next best thing and thanked Terry for the impact her life has had on mine. Terry's response: "It really did remind me that maybe I'm not all used up after all. I just might have something to give".

Leave Your Mark

Dear friend, your life is leaving a mark on the world. Your handprints are all over the place. Someone is walking in your footsteps. The words you speak echo loud and long in halls and hearts and the ripple of your life continues long after your days on this earth end.

We live in a world where people are famous for being ruthless, or famous for being rude, or famous for being immoral, or famous for being famous. It's not surprising when we consider who the prince of this world is. But the King of Kings is still on the throne and in His kingdom what makes one great is quite different. He's told us clearly in His Word.

Greatness = Service

Service is:
A listening ear
Preparing a meal
Caring for a child, a parent, or even a pet
Mowing a lawn
Repairing a car
Financial assistance
And so much more

The list is long and as diverse as the human race. We are each uniquely gifted to serve.

Greatness is better than fame. Fame is short lived. Fame can be bought. And not everyone can be famous. Greatness ripples through eternity. The circle of one's influence grows wider each year as one life touches another. And everyone, including you, can be great.

Takeaway Truth

"But whoever would be great among you must be your servant, and whoever would be first among you must be your slave, even as the Son of Man came not to be served but to serve, and to give his life as a ransom for many." (Matt 20:26-28)

6

When You Want to Have a Servant's Heart

When we meet someone for the first time we ask, "So what do you do?" The response usually includes a job title, position, or current activity. I've identified as an athlete, a student, minister, wife, mother, teacher, writer, and runner depending on my season of life. But here's the problem: what happens to my identity when I can no longer *do* something? Who am I if I lose my title or position or the ability to do my thing?

In the previous chapter, I said that greatness is achieved by being a servant. I didn't make that up. Jesus taught it and proved it with His life. What I had to learn the hard way about greatness and service is this: serving isn't just about what I do for someone; it's also about who I am—my identity. And if my identity isn't rooted in Christ then my service is just busyness propped up by pride.

Years ago, I had a friend who was in the process of losing his job. He came and talked to me and said, "If I'm not a _________, I'm nothing." As a young woman in my twenties I remember thinking how sad it must be to have your whole identity wrapped up in your current job title. A hard lesson was just around the corner for me. Isn't it always? A few, short years later I found myself struggling with the same issue. My choice to leave professional ministry to be a full-time stay-at-home mom left me asking "Who am I?" and struggling to answer the so-what-do-you-do question. It would take a few years and some divine encounters to understand that my true identity is rooted in Christ.

One encounter profoundly changed my life. We were in a new church and a couple had graciously invited us out to dinner. It was obvious that the man was a successful businessman but we didn't know the specifics of his work. Over coffee I asked, "So what do you do?" His response: "I'm a cheerleader." He went on to explain how he did that but never mentioned his business or his company name. As we got to know him and his family better his true identity became apparent when his business hit a low point during the recession. He continued to serve by being a cheerleader. His identify wasn't rooted in his job title, his bank account, or his accomplishments. He understood his role as a child of God, so whether business was booming or the bottom was falling out, he was a cheerleader in service to Almighty God. Still, when I encounter him, he is always cheering for me on my journey.

My mother was a servant. She served her family, church, and community though she always preferred to work behind the scenes. She loved to share her home and her home-cooking with whomever dropped by. She never had a job title but she was always serving—doing something for others. The last three months of her life were spent in a hospital bed unable to do anything for anyone. She was unable even to care for herself but she served until her final days. From her bed, she faithfully proclaimed the grace and mercy of a loving God who had given her all her days, even the ones marred by disease. Visitors poured in eager to see her one more time, to be served by her one last time. Her deep understanding of servanthood and her identity in Christ made being in her presence a joy and a blessing. She never expressed a need to "do something"; she never spoke of hopelessness or helplessness. Being a servant wasn't just something she did when she was able; it was who she had become as she rested in Christ.

Do you have a servant's heart or are you just busy?

How do you identify?

How to Know if You Have a Servant's Heart

1. Remove the audience. If no one knows about or appreciates your service and you don't feel the need to mention it you have a servant's heart. If you seldom worry or complain about being forgotten or overlooked you have a servant's heart.

2. Remove the ability or opportunity to do something. If you're content when there's nothing you can *do*, you might have a servant's heart. If you don't feel helpless when you can't help, you might have a servant's heart. You're available and ready for your next assignment from God and content to wait on Him.

I. Still. Struggle. With. This. I am a do-er, a fix-er, and a helper. I like my hard work to be noticed and appreciated. I hate feeling helpless.

Doing is good. It really is. I'll never stop doing what I can but our identity must be rooted in Christ, not in what we can do. Service done by the power of the Holy Spirit is a blessing and God gets the glory. Deeds done apart from Him, no matter how noble they appear, may be more of a burden for everyone.

Service leads to joy. Busyness leaves us resentful. I've flopped and flailed and pushed pride to center stage enough to know that what you do isn't what matters most. An identity rooted in Christ alone---now that's a servant's heart He can use!

Takeaway Truth

"I have been crucified with Christ. It is no longer I who live, but Christ who lives in me. And the life I now live in the flesh I live by faith in the Son of God, who loved me and gave himself for me." (Gal 2:20)

7

When You Need a Solution

What's your problem? Whatever it is, you might approach it in one of two ways:

1. Surrender to the nagging feeling that the tide of battle has shifted against you and admit that you're fairly powerless to do anything about it.

or

2. Fight with the battle cry, "I can handle it on my own."

Wrong and wrong. Neither approach is the best way. As Christ followers, we need not surrender as victims or fight in self-sufficiency. There's a better way.

In Exodus 17:8-13, the Amalekites attacked the Israelites. Moses instructs Joshua to prepare the men for battle. As they fight Moses stands on a hill overlooking the battlefield and prays with arms outstretched to heaven. The Israelite troops prevail. But as Moses's arms grow weary and fall, the battle shifts and the enemy begins to prevail. He must keep his arms outstretched toward heaven in prayer if he wants to open the door for God's supernatural intervention on the battlefield.

Prayer is the better way to approach a problem. Prayer is the key to victory in every battle.

The Right Way to Approach a Problem

1. Pray. If you're willing to invite God to involve himself in your daily challenges, you will experience His prevailing power---in your home, in your relationships, in the marketplace, in the schools, in the church---wherever it is most needed.

2. Pray with and for others. There's always a battle raging somewhere for someone. Remember to come alongside another whose arms may be weary and hold them up in prayer. You'll get to share the victory.

So often I stay too long on the battlefield, doing my part to defeat the enemy. I get wounded and weary. When there's a need for a solution, a commitment to prayer calls me to the hill overlooking the battlefield. I stand with others, arms outstretched toward heaven, inviting God to intervene. I can see the battle from a different perspective when I pray and I'm reminded that I need to come to the hill overlooking the battlefield more often.

God's prevailing power is released in my life (and yours) when we pray.

> Prayerless people cut themselves off from God's prevailing power, and the frequent result is the familiar feeling of being overwhelmed, overrun, beaten down, pushed around, defeated. Surprising numbers of people are willing to settle for lives like that.[1]

Takeaway Truth

"Is anyone among you suffering? Let him pray." (James 5:13)

8

When You Come Face to Face With Your Baggage

"God doesn't just want the best part of you---the part you've polished and prettied up with a fancy bow. He desires the worst parts of us most of all---the parts we despise, the parts we are afraid of, the parts we most want to hide from the world, from our own selves, and from Him. He even wants the part of us that doesn't have faith or trust in Him."
Michelle DeRusha, True You

"God wants the worst parts of us most of all." Really? I still struggle to believe that after all these years as a Christ follower. I mean, I can talk and write about it passionately and tell you it's true for you, while doubting it's true for me. Deep in my soul, I doubt it's true for me. I've always had the feeling that I needed to prove my worth---my value---to the world, and even to God.

Of course, I know all the Bible verses that tell me otherwise. Two of my favorites are:

"But God shows his love for us in that while we were still sinners, Christ died for us." (Rom 5:8)

"There is therefore now no condemnation for those who are in Christ Jesus." (Rom 8:1)

I want you to know if you ever feel like you're not enough, or you've done too much, or God couldn't possibly want you, I feel the same way sometimes. I feel that way often. I feel that way at some point every day. I think I was born feeling that way because I can hardly remember a time that I didn't.

Facing My Baggage with Faith

Faith carries me through those times. They're hard and dark times for sure but I don't know what I would do, how I would live and get through a day, without the belief that there is someone bigger than me and all my doubts.

I know the shame of being told, "You just need to have more faith" so that you don't feel that way anymore. Okay. Well, that sounds a whole lot like, "You need to do better and try harder."

I've been around that mountain enough times to know this: if doing better and trying harder could save me I wouldn't need Jesus. But I do need Him. And you need Him, too. He knows the worst parts of us so He knows how desperately we need Him.

I've found that when I talk to God with brutal honesty about my doubts and fears and unbelief, He gives healing and clarity and greater faith.

Even those who through grace can say, "Lord, I believe," have reason to complain of their unbelief. We cannot always readily apply it to ourselves or depend upon it, as we should. In our unbelief, we must look up to Christ for grace to help us against it. His grace is sufficient. His strength is perfected in our weakness.

Takeaway Truth

"Immediately the father of the child cried out and said, 'I believe; help my unbelief!'" (Mark 9:24)

9

When You Long for Purpose and Connection

In my life I've had two ongoing struggles: purpose and connection. I share this because I know I'm not the only one. Every week I talk to individuals who wonder, "Am I doing what I'm supposed to do, what I was created to do?" These same people also express a desire to connect with others in a meaningful way. These concerns are born out of our need to make the most of the life we've been given.

We Are Image-Bearers

I believe the desire for purpose and connection is central to our existence as image-bearers. The Word of God reveals these facts.

1. God is a God of purpose.

He purposes for us to have a purpose: “For I know the plans I have for you, declares the Lord, plans for welfare and not for evil, to give you a future and a hope.” (Jer 29:11)

He purposes for us to be saved: “This is good, and it is pleasing in the sight of God our Savior, who desires all people to be saved and to come to the knowledge of the truth.” (I Tim 2:3-4)

He purposes for us to be like Him: “For this is the will of God, your sanctification.” (I Thess 4:3)

He purposes for us to be thankful: “Give thanks in all circumstances; for this is the will of God in Christ Jesus for you.” (I Thess 5:18)

2. God values connection with us:

The names of God reveal, among other things, His relational character. He is Creator, Redeemer, Master, Teacher, Comforter, and Healer, just to name a few; and each of those names depicts a way in which the God of the Universe relates to His children.

He says to us: "I will make my dwelling among you, and my soul shall not abhor you. And I will walk among you and will be your God, and you shall be my people." (Lev 26:11-12)

He invites: "Come to me, all who labor and are heavy laden, and I will give you rest." (Matt 11:28)

Over and over the Lord invites us, commands even, that we call out to Him and depend on Him for our every need. We were created in the image of our Maker by our Maker for His purpose.

For years I labeled myself a "people-pleaser" until the Lord helped me see that what my soul really longs for is connection and meaningful relationships. In my search for purpose and my need to connect with others I've made the same mistakes over and over:

I wrongly assume two things:

1. Discovering my purpose starts with me. I assume I need to take a test, read the newest book, know my personality type, and get myself figured out once and for all and then I'll know my purpose.

2. Connecting with others in a meaningful way has to be big and newsworthy. I assume my purpose involves single-handedly changing the world.

Both of these assumptions are lies I tell myself and/or lies from the Enemy. There's certainly nothing inherently sinful about taking personality tests or reading books in order to understand human nature but the sin is elevating those activities above the knowledge of God.

There's a line in the movie *Under the Tuscan Sun* where Katherine says to Frances, "When I was a little girl, I used to run around in the fields all day, trying unsuccessfully to catch ladybugs. Finally, I would get tired and lay down for a nap. When I awoke, I'd find ladybugs walking all over me."[1]

This reminds me of how often in my search for a life of purpose and meaningful connection, I miss the life of purpose and people to connect with right in front of me.

In your search for purpose and connection, don't miss your purpose with the people right in front of you. Thankfully, the God of Purpose and Connection does not sit by and do nothing. He knows our deepest needs, the desires of our heart. He is always at work showing Himself strong on our behalf for His glory.

An Ordinary Day

On an ordinary day, while I'm sitting in a fan-filled football stadium, God pulls back the curtain of my life and gives me a glimpse into His purpose fulfilled in and through me. The music blares loud as I watch families file in and sit all around me. They juggle programs, hot dogs, and small children. I watch the sunset and notice how storm clouds highlight beauty.

And then out of the thousands of voices around me, the Spirit highlights one behind me of a man I didn't know very well a few weeks ago.

I remember the day I got the phone call. I was at home folding laundry and feeling small when a leader at my church called to say, "Do you know ___________?"

I sat down from my work and responded with, "I know who you're talking about but I don't really know him."

"Okay," he said. "I'm calling because I've suggested to him that he come to the Sunday morning small group Bible study that you and Eric lead."

"Okay. That's great! We'd love to have him and I believe he'll enjoy the sweet fellowship of our small group."

He came that Sunday and has continued to be involved in the life of our church.

Sidebar:

Teaching Sunday School is my ordinary. I've been doing it almost every Sunday, all my adult life. Fifteen or so men and women meet in a room each week for an hour, with chairs arranged in a U-shape. We drink from Styrofoam coffee cups, tell funny stories, share prayer requests, open the Bible, and consider together what God wants to teach us and how we're to apply it to our lives right now.

The man who came to Sunday School heard about a support group we lead and started attending it each week.

Sidebar:

Leading a support group is our ordinary. It's part of our training and something we've done for years. Each week a handful of people meet in a small room and sit in a circle with cups of coffee or water. We find hope and healing as we share our stories with one another.

Saturday, as we walked toward the stadium with dozens of other people, we ran into him. We walked to the stadium together chatting about the heat of September in the South. As we approached the gate we went our separate ways.

Sidebar:

Sitting at a college football game on Saturday evening isn't my ordinary. Those who know me well know I like to stay home on Saturday night. It's the beginning of my Sabbath rest. I love to watch college football but going to a ballgame wasn't on my list of things to do during my Saturday evening Sabbath. I even suggested to the guys that I stay at home and do my thing while they go and enjoy the game. They really wanted me to go so I did.

All these seemingly random, ordinary and not-so-ordinary events of the past month went through my mind as I considered how we ended up sitting together in a stadium of over 20,000 people. This man, who was a relative stranger just a month ago, is now a friend. I know a part of his story, his struggle, and the losses that weigh heavy. He knows mine, too. We've laughed and cried together and testified to the hope we have in Christ.

I'm still soaking in the sacred moment of a Saturday college football game, watching a stormy sunset, and realizing how God is always at work fulfilling His purposes and making connections through a phone call, a small group, a family outing, a chance meeting, and a sunset.

Can you see His hand at work in your own life, too?

Through all of this, I'm reminded of the wise words of Elisabeth Elliot: “When you don’t know what to do next, just do the thing in front of you.”

God Is At Work

In a culture obsessed with celebrity and novelty, emotional highs and experiences, we’ve forgotten that real life is mostly lived in the daily mundane. It’s not lived on mountaintops and it’s not impressive enough to be a Facebook status. It’s a series of uncelebrated steps, of hidden habits. This week you’ll do a hundred unspectacular things: brush your teeth, eat food, wash dishes, do laundry, answer the phone, pay bills, gas up your car, wash your hands, make your bed, etc.

God has often written His story in the midst of everyday affairs. He is always, always at work in us and around us and He wants to work through us. He is weaving Himself into our lives and weaving us together with one another as the Body of Christ.

Takeaway Truth

"Give thanks in all circumstances; for this is the will of God in Christ Jesus for you." (I Thess 5:18)

10

When You've Lost Your Way

You've probably seen the quote "All who wander are not lost." That may be true but sometimes I wonder if I've wandered too far.

I remember the last time I was lost. We were driving to a party at a friend's house. I was sure I knew how to get where were going. I'd been in that part of town several times but just to be safe we followed the directions from the GPS. We soon realized we were lost, at night, in the rain, listening to Country Christmas music.

After several unsuccessful attempts to find our way we decided to phone a friend. I was so relieved when she answered. She helped us get back on the right road and talked us through the winding roads and signs along the way. When we made a wrong turn she helped us see we weren't quite there yet. She encouraged us to keep going and stayed with me on the phone until we had safely reached our destination. She was sympathetic to the trouble the storm had caused and understood how easy it was to lose our way in the dark. She was just the voice I needed to hear.

This wasn't the first time I've lost my way. Life is full of storms and dark places.

Often I think I know the way. "I've been here before," I tell myself. So I keep going, wandering and wondering, down the wrong road. The consequences are grave. I risk missing the abundant life. (John 10:10). But our Father is sympathetic to the trouble the storm can cause and He understands how easy it is to lose our way in this dark world. So He gives clear instructions about what we're to do when we've lost our way.

When you've lost your way do this:

1. Stop! Acknowledge (confess) that you're on the wrong path. Thus says the Lord: “Cursed is the man who trusts in man and makes flesh his strength, whose heart turns away from the Lord.” (Jer 17:5)

2. Look! Seek out a reliable source of truth--God's Word. “I will instruct you and teach you in the way you should go; I will counsel you with my eye upon you. ‘ (Ps 32:8)

3. Listen! Follow the instructions you are given. “Thus says the Lord, your Redeemer, the Holy One of Israel: ‘I am the Lord your God, who teaches you to profit, who leads you in the way you should go.’” (Is 48:17)

No matter how far you’ve wandered, you’re never too far gone for God.

Takeaway Truth

“We must all die; we are like water spilled on the ground, which cannot be gathered up again. But God will not take away life, and he devises means so that the banished one will not remain an outcast.” (2 Sam 14:14)

11

When You've Lost Your Joy

Have you ever had a season of joylessness? I sure have. Even as a mature Christian I've had times in my life when I just didn't have the joy I once had. But I believe there's a prescription---a remedy to restore the joy we've lost.

His Name Was Jealous

On a trip to Zambia, Africa in 2016, I had the privilege of attending church at Mufutuli Vineyard Ministries. "Mufutuli" means Savior and "Vineyard" refers to the farm that provides food and funds for the church, orphanage, and school Pastor Charles Simoonga and his wife, Mary, began years ago. It's a beautiful, life-giving place.

The church's meeting place is what we would refer to as a large shed with walls made of cardboard and thatch. The service has just begun as our team arrives and a young man leads the congregation in a call to worship. His rich voice guides and the congregation echoes. His joy is contagious. I watch women-wearing-babies, precious orphans, and men crippled by disease worship with eyes fixed on him and hearts on Him. He claps and sways and marches from one side of the congregation to the other. It's a cool morning but flushed cheeks and sweat drops reveal the work in his worship.

There are no instruments. None are needed. The language is unfamiliar yet my heart beats with praise. We are one, these strangers and me.

After the service, Pastor Charles and I stand shoulder to shoulder on dusty, holy ground and the joy-full worship leader walks up. I introduce myself and shake his hand.

He says, "Nice to meet you. My name is Jealous."

Before I can catch my thoughts these words fly: "No! Your name is Joy! You are Joy!" He laughs shyly.

Pastor Charles speaks up. "Tell her your testimony."

I'll never forget the look on his face as he inhaled grace. Very somberly, in his thick South African accent, he said, "I was stealing, fighting, drinking, and using many women. I was a very, very bad man." Then a smile as wide as the ocean broke across his face as he says, "But I met Pastor Charles and then I met Jesus."

I grab the dark hands of my brother in Christ, "And that's why you have joy. You ARE Joy!"

He nods and replies, "Yes! Yes. Yes."

I see him several times throughout our trip and each time I greet him, "Hello, Joy." He nods and smiles in agreement.

On our last day at the farm I see him talking to Pastor Charles. As I approach them to say "Goodbye" Pastor Charles says, "He going to try and have his name legally changed from Jealous to Joy."

I hug him and say, "Because of Jesus, that's who you really are."

Where Joy Comes From

It's important to remember that joy is a fruit of the Holy Spirit produced by God's work in us. Joy is a gift from God and the response we bear as we become aware of His grace. We can have joy even in the most difficult circumstances because of the Holy Spirit. But I know from experience that even in the best of circumstances, joy can feel like a forgotten memory.

Job, David, and Elijah all experienced joylessness. You and I know the feeling. The good news is that we don't have to remain joyless. God's Word offers us some guidelines for when we've lost our joy.

What to Do When You've Lost Your Joy

1. Focus. Focus on God. Think about God. Read about God. Talk about God. Sing about God. He is the source of your joy as a believer. I've often made the mistake of over-thinking my joylessness. "Why am I joyless? How did I get here? What went wrong?" We get more of what we focus on. If we focus on our joylessness we get more joylessness. Focus on God and find your joy.

Read Psalm 118.

2. Pray. Talk to God. It's easy to slip into the habit of telling others our troubles, fears, and frustrations but I've found rehearsing those aloud with others breeds joylessness. Confess your joylessness to the only One who can restore joy. Ask Him for what you need.

Read Philippians 4:6-7

3. Think. Think about what you're thinking about. You have the ability to control what you think. While unpleasant thoughts may slip into your mind you don't have to let them stay. Choose what you think about, choose good thoughts, and you'll change your life.

Read Philippians 4:8

4. Obey. Make it your habit to follow the commands of God given in the Bible. I've found that one of my greatest sources of joylessness is disobedience. When you pray, ask God to reveal any unconfessed sin in your life and repent. As a believer, we will never know the joy of the Lord if we live in disobedience.

Read Genesis 4:7

5. Connect. Spend time with joyful believers. Seek out those who bear the fruit of the Holy Spirit. Fellowship with believers who are intentional about growing in their faith.

Read Hebrews 10:19-25

If you've met Jesus then you have everything you need to have joy---to be Joy.

Takeaway Truth

"Though you have not seen him, you love him. Though you do not now see him, you believe in him and rejoice with joy that is inexpressible and filled with glory, obtaining the outcome of your faith, the salvation of your souls." (I Pet 1:8-9)

12

When It Feels Like Everything is Falling Apart

My daughter, Maddie, shared with me what she had written in her journal after a few particularly difficult weeks. I was greatly encouraged by her words and with her permission share them here.

Falling Apart

As most of us have figured out, life doesn't always go as planned. Relationships are strained, classes are hard, and work is stressful. Going into every situation I want to know the outcome and I work as hard as I can to make the outcome go according to my plan. I want all my relationships to be easy, I want to get A's in all my classes, and I hope for a stress-free workday. When I drop one of the balls I'm juggling I immediately feel like everything is falling apart. When things aren't going my way I'm discontent.

I'm certain I'm not the only one who feels this way.

Here's my story:

Over the past couple of years, I've reached a milestone every six months. I graduated high school and got a new job. I quit my job and moved to New Orleans, found a church, made new friends, and settled into my new home.

For most of us a new year is filled with joyful anticipation of a new beginning. We get busy making resolutions and plans. However, during one particular season I was feeling "less-than" and had no motivation to start or accomplish anything.

I had the “I just want to run away” feeling many times. I felt as though I was floating aimlessly through life. In my mind, nothing I did mattered. I'd convinced myself that nothing would change if I weren't here. I had no intention of harming myself, but I was sure if I disappeared no one would notice.

To add to the list, I'd fallen into the trap of looking to the internet and TV to answer life’s questions and solve my problems. I found plenty of information telling me how I should look, what job I should have, how much money I should make, how my relationships should be, and, of course, what I need to be doing to be considered successful---which is really just code for "you need to do more."

Before I knew it, I couldn’t even discern truth anymore. Even though I was reading God’s Word daily, I'd allowed the voice of the world to be louder than the voice of the Creator. The thought of abandoning my calling because I won’t make money and feeling like I should sign-up for everything so that I feel useful were constantly invading my mind.

I'd lose sleep worrying about something I heard in a movie or something I watched on YouTube. I replayed something I read on Facebook with a title like “6 Ways to Look More Attractive in Pictures” or “15 Things Only the Most Amazing Girlfriends Do”. I'm ashamed to admit that I've read these articles but that's how damaged my thought life had become. I'd convinced myself that the people who wrote these articles must know everything and therefore it was absolutely necessary for me to read it so that I could stay in the know. These articles and others like them wreaked havoc in my life in more ways than one. Anxiety and mild depression began to consume me. I'd never dealt with anything like this and I couldn’t figure out what was causing it.

I spent months waking up every hour wondering how I could fit all these rules and suggestions into my life so that it could be better. Every morning my playlist sounded something like this:

I need to lose weight

I should probably dye my hair so that I can fit in

I need to make more money

I'm not a good friend.

I'm not a good girlfriend (based on the article I read)

I need to start dressing like ____ so that I won’t look so ____.

I need to start going out more so I’ll have friends.

And the list goes on and on.

Looking Up

During this difficult season, the New Orleans weather was perfect. There were warm days with lots of sunshine and a cool, gulf breeze. One day I was on my way to the cafeteria when I looked up.

What I saw took my breath away and the Lord spoke a sweet message into my heart. I realized that my problems and worries are not as big of a deal as I was making them out to be. I want to control every aspect of my life but creation reminds me that God is in control.

The gulf breeze doesn't blow because of my design and trees do not sway at my command. Birds don't sing because I gave them a voice nor do the flowers bloom because I say so.

My struggle came down to one thing: I wasn't content. I was constantly trying to micromanage every aspect of the rest of my life. I was trying to fix situations that hadn't even happened yet.

But I'm learning to be satisfied with my current circumstances instead of trying to control what will happen ten years from now or even tomorrow. I am practicing gratefulness, naming things I am grateful for in place of every single thing I'm tempted to worry about. Doing this has completely changed my outlook.

So, instead of worrying about what we *don't* have or what *could* happen, we can choose to focus on what we do have and what God is doing in each moment of our lives and the lives of others.

Jesus made the ultimate sacrifice for us because it was something we couldn't do on our own. When I'm tempted to carry everything on my own I'm reminded that not only am I unable, but I don't have to. My significance is not based on my abilities or titles but in Jesus Christ alone. When we look for our identity in our circumstances or accomplishments we will always be disappointed. But when we look for our identity in Christ our hope is unshakeable.

Takeaway Truth

"But we have this treasure in jars of clay, to show that the surpassing power belongs to God and not to us. We are afflicted in every way, but not crushed; perplexed, but not driven to despair; persecuted, but not forsaken; struck down, but not destroyed; always carrying in the body the death of Jesus, so that the life of Jesus may also be manifested in our bodies.” (2 Cor 4:7-10)

13

When You Feel Undone

I'm a list person. I make grocery lists, to-do lists, and lists of people to call. I make a list for cleaning, packing, and decorating. I make lists on notepads, napkins, sticky-notes, receipts, and church bulletins. I've even considered making a master list of lists.

All these lists have one thing in common. They're all undone. Not one list is ever finished, with all items checked off. The undoneness haunts me. Sometimes I am tempted to throw the list away and forget about what's left undone. Sometimes I do. But the undone thing is left hanging in my mind like a loose thread. I make a new list and add it there hoping that I can mark it off as "done". I've even added tasks I've completed to my list just so I could mark them off as "done". I need that kind of closure.

But it's really not the undone lists that get me most. They are perhaps a reminder that I am undone.

At brief moments I may feel done. But soon, something or someone comes along and presents something that is my un-doing. A word, a memory, a missed appointment, a loss---and I am undone---again.

With the prophet Isaiah I can say, "Woe is me! For I am undone," (Isa 6:5) What was his undoing?

> In this figurative vision, the temple is thrown open to view, even to the most holy place. The prophet, standing outside the temple, sees the Divine Presence seated on the mercy-seat, raised over the ark of the covenant, between the cherubim and seraphim, and the Divine glory filled the whole

> temple...This awful vision of the Divine Majesty overwhelmed the prophet with a sense of his own vileness A glimpse of heavenly glory is enough to convince us that all our righteousnesses are as filthy rags.[1]

Filthy rags? Is that it? Am I left undone?

"The thief comes only to kill, steal, and destroy." (John 10:10) Undone. Matthew Henry says, "We are undone if there is not a Mediator between us and this holy God."[2]

The rest of John 10:10 reveals the Mediator, Jesus, who said, "I have come that they may have life and have it to the full." Done.

Gary Morland tells a story in his book, *Scary Hope*:

> One day I came home from work and she was reading a book. She held it out to me, pointed to a page and said, "Is this true?" It was something about the finished work that Jesus Christ accomplished on the cross, not just for heaven, but for here, right now.
>
> "Oh, yeah, that's true."
>
> That was the moment everything changed.
>
> A supernatural peace was born in her. It was a silent, unspectacular turning point. She became a woman of grace, instinctively trusting the sufficiency of Jesus Christ for everyday living. She had been a Christian for twenty-five years, but still believed there was something left undone in her.
>
> Then God personally showed her, in a way I still don't understand, that all her un-dones were done on the cross with Jesus.[3]

All my undones are done. With Jesus' death on the cross, God finished what He started. He marked off several things on His list.

5 Things Christ Accomplished by His Death:

<u>1. Removed our sin and guilt. Check.</u>

2. Removed His wrath without sacrificing His justice and holiness. Check.

3. Removed our alienation from Him. Check.

4. Delivered us from the captivity of sin. Check.

5. Defeated the power of Satan. Check.

Jesus did all of this by dying in our place. My place. Your place. We are done. We are done because Jesus said, "It is finished" and I believe Him.

Today, I will make a list. Tonight, it will be undone. But I am choosing to trust the sufficiency of the finished work of Jesus Christ in my life.

Will you?

Takeaway Truth

"There is therefore now no condemnation for those who are in Christ Jesus." (Romans 8:1)

14

When You Need the Unforced Rhythms of Grace

I'm proud to have been raised with a strong work ethic. To this day hard work is one of the things I value most.

There are many benefits associated with hard work and I'm thankful to enjoy and share the fruits of my labor. But through the years I've become a pro at "burning the candle at both ends". My solution to a problem often starts with "work harder" and ends with a gold star on my image-maintenance report card. I've been guilty of wearing worn-out and weary like a badge of honor as I strive to prove myself and polish my identity. And I have been wrong--sinful even---as I distort God's plan.

We are always on the clock. Truth be told our work is never done. We go to work, take care of our home and garden, go to meetings and appointments, carpool and wait, and all the while we're making a mental inventory of the pantry, the laundry room, the inbox, and the bank account. And if we aren't careful we can begin to grow bitter in our work.

He created and designed us to be workers---hard workers even. Work is not a punishment but a gift. So is rest. This is beautifully illustrated in the first chapter of Genesis when we see God at work. He worked (created), called it "good", and rested. There is a lovely rhythm to his work and his rest. He is teaching me.

I am learning that a Sabbath day, Sunday for most of us, doesn't guarantee rest from our work. Someone gave me a coffee cup that says, "I need a day between Saturday and Sunday." You know the feeling, right? But we may also feel we need an actual day of rest between Sunday and Monday. We'll never get those extra days.

The answer---the cure for our soul-weariness---is a Sabbath heart. We must learn to embrace the rest of God. A Sabbath day won't feel restful until we have a Sabbath heart. And a Sabbath heart will create a rhythm, allowing us to rest in Him anytime, anywhere, every day of the week.

There's more going on than our eyes can see and our ears can hear. All the words, save for His Word, are skewed, biased and purposeful. We're in danger of dying from distraction. We're the redeemable refusing the rescue.

The Conspirator seeks to steal, kill, and destroy. Perhaps we're unknowingly aiding and abetting the Enemy. He offers swift victory and quick fixes. He promises we'll be known and liked, accomplished and successful.

Guard your heart! Awake, O Sleeper! Gird up your mind. Put on and employ the full armor of God. Allow Him to inhabit your existence without remainder. Let Him fill you until there's nothing left over.

A Sabbath heart. God in the midst of the silence, solitude, and stillness. One writer describes a Sabbath heart like this:

> The trained ability to be fully present and wholly awake in order to discover or rediscover the simplest things---the in and out of our breathing, the coolness of tiles on our bare feet, the way the wind sculpts clouds into crocodiles and polar bears.[1]

When was the last time you sat still and upright in silence---noticing the birdsong in the trees or the squirrel that lightly gallops across your roof? No TV. No music. No vibrating, dinging, ringing phone.

Would you notice the geese on their early morning fly over?

When was the last time you stepped barefoot onto wet grass---on purpose? And instead of cringing and complaining and regretting, you embrace the awakening of all your senses? The damp, cold shiver. The soft, soaked earth.

Have you lost the childlike wonder of holding water in cupped hands? Soft and clear, it cleanses and soothes tired joints.

But we sabotage our Sabbath rest.
We work only to finish.
We read only to inform.
We cook only to eat.
We give only to get.
We walk only to track steps.
We dress to impress.

What if we embraced the possibility of working and reading, cooking and giving, walking and dressing with no agenda or pretense? What if our highest goal was joyful rest?

The One full of grace and truth dwells among us---in us. Do you know His rhythm? Lean in, bend your ears and eyes and heart and mind to know and rest in his rhythm.

Oh! What the unforced rhythms of grace offer!

Takeaway Truth

"And the Word became flesh and dwelt among us, and we have seen his glory, glory as of the only Son from the Father, full of grace and truth." (John 1:14)

15

When Your Heart is a Tangled Mess

At 2:00 a.m. I slip out of bed and feel my way toward the bathroom. The room is dark and I like it that way but my third toe finds the chair at the end of my bed. Ouch! I make it to the bathroom and flip the light on. My toe is still attached to my foot. I thought it might not be.

I walk slowly to the kitchen, get a glass of water, and sit on the sofa. How do I feel? Sick from the throbbing toe you ask? (You would think so if you could see it now.) It does hurt and I think it might be broken. But it's not what I'm thinking about or feeling. In the wee hours of the morning, sitting on the sofa with a throbbing toe, my heart beats to the rhythm of rejection.

Rejection

It is the exact single word that comes to my mind as soon as I sit down. The darkness is heavy but not like the feeling in my chest. I cry out the truth I know.

"O Lord, you have searched me and known me!
You know when I sit down and when I rise up;
you discern my thoughts from afar.
You search out my path and my lying down
and are acquainted with all my ways.
Even before a word is on my tongue,
behold, O Lord, you know it altogether." (Ps 139: 1-4)

I'm barely awake but deeply troubled. My heart is tangled in a mess of lies and half-truths.

"Child, unwind yourself from that thing. Wrap yourself around Me," He says.

I pull the blanket tighter around my shoulders. He begins to reveal other things that entangle me. I don't want to think about it. I want to go back to bed. I'll think about it tomorrow I reason.

"Where shall I go from your Spirit?
  Or where shall I flee from your presence?
If I ascend to heaven, you are there!
  If I make my bed in Sheol, you are there!
If I take the wings of the morning
  and dwell in the uttermost parts of the sea,
even there your hand shall lead me,
  and your right hand shall hold me.
If I say, "Surely the darkness shall cover me,
  and the light about me be night,"
even the darkness is not dark to you;
  the night is bright as the day,
  for darkness is as light with you." (Ps 139: 7-12)

How easy it is to get wrapped up in the wrong thing---beauty, success, a person, an expectation, __________ (you fill in the blank). They may have a place and a purpose in this world but when I get all wrapped up in anything other than God my heart becomes a tangled mess: rejected, duped, played, and empty.

"Search me, O God, and know my heart!
  Try me and know my thoughts!
And see if there be any grievous way in me,
  and lead me in the way everlasting!" (Ps 139: 23-24)

Even if it's in the middle of the night.

I sit alone with Him for another hour. The room is dark but now I can see the lie and feel the Light. That's what truth does for us and to us.

Takeaway Truth

"Your word is a lamp to my feet and a light to my path." (Ps 119:105)

16

When You Can't Sleep

A battle is raging in and around me. I'm fighting to break free from clutter, sugar, fear, and a few other things that I won't name here. There seems to be no end to it all and the fiery darts of the Enemy are coming hard from every direction. I need to be fully awake, physically and spiritually. And there's the rub. I'm sleepless in the battle.

As instructed I've put on the full armor of God and I'm clinging to the promise that we are more than conquerors through Him who loved us. But this warrior needs a nap! If you're struggling to get a good night's sleep, too, then maybe what I'm learning will help.

Sleepless in the Battle

I couldn't sleep last night. I went to bed on time and fell asleep fairly quickly. But I didn't stay asleep. Not long after midnight I woke up and stayed awake for several hours. This is fairly normal for me. I've never been a "good sleeper". I blame it on years of late-night studying in my 20's, restless babies in my 30's, and menopause in my 40's. I blame it on caffeine, spicy food, and a bad mattress.

Sometimes I recall Bible verses or grab my earbuds and open my Bible app to the Book of Psalms. Sometimes I get up and watch TV. And sometimes I just lie there and rehearse the undone list, the mistakes I've made, and attempt to solve all my problems. The "what-if and how will I" questions overwhelm me. Melatonin is the strongest thing I've ever tried and I'm pretty sure sweet tarts would've been more effective.

Please, don't misunderstand what I'm trying to say. I'm not making light of sleeplessness. From what I can tell, it's a big problem for people of all ages and all walks of life. No one seems to have a definitive solution. In my case, I've come to the conclusion that instead of blaming menopause or my mattress or getting a sleep study or a pill, I need to wake up and realize something else is going on.

Now I Lay Me Down To Sleep

"If I'll quieten my mind, I'll go back to sleep," I think to myself as the clock ticks and night slips into morning. "I need more sleep," I argue as I calculate how much sleep I've actually gotten and how much I could get if I fall asleep this very minute. I lie still and attempt to clear my mind and control my breathing.

"I need to talk to you," I hear my Father say.

"Breathe. Relax your muscles. Clear your mind," I tell myself again.

"I want to talk to you now," He insists.

"Okay, I'm listening, Lord" I think as I roll over , flip my pillow to the cold side again, and stare into the darkness.

"Get up. Get out of bed."

"Ugh!"

I go to the bathroom first and then quietly slip out of the bedroom, closing the door gently behind me. At least someone's sleeping tonight. (He has his sleepless nights, too.)

The hallway nightlight and the sweet scent of warm vanilla welcome me. With a cup of cold water in hand, I sink down into my favorite chair. I'm tempted to pick up a book or my Bible and read myself to sleep. Maybe I should fold the laundry?

"Be still," He says as I sip cold water.

So I am. Still. Quiet. Alone in His Presence. I'm not counting the minutes or looking at the clock. Time stands still and so do I.

Listen Up

"I will bless the LORD who guides me; even at night, my heart instructs me." (Ps 16:7)

I used to think this verse meant that God would speak to us while we sleep. I believe He does. I know for certain He has spoken to me while I slept. But also I think it means that He counsels us at night, perhaps when we think we should be sleeping.

The Psalmist didn't think it unusual to lie awake at night. He knew what to do during those sleepless nights. "I remember you upon my bed, and meditate on you in the watches of the night." (Ps 63:6)

Sometimes God wants to talk to me and sometimes He just wants to be with me. He knows I need to be with Him.

Do we even know how to just be with?

Perhaps the reason we can't power down our brain at night is that we never power down our brain. Ever. We're stuck in the "on" position and "on" always means high alert. We see and read and hear too much all day long and think and overthink our life and friends' lives and the lives of people we've never met. And perhaps our only problem isn't overthinking sleeplessness, but how we spend our sleepless nights.

For most of us, the middle of the night and the wee hours of the morning are the only times we can actually be still and quiet and alone with God. Life is hectic and noisy. So often when we're "spending time with God" we're in a crowded sanctuary or behind the wheel of a car, or with a devotional book in our lap. We group worship and group study and group pray. Jesus was a people-person but He knew He needed time alone with God.

Time.

Alone.

With the Father.

Many times during his life, Jesus went away to a quiet place to be alone with His Father. He valued time with God more than food or sleep. He stepped away from working miracles and teaching because His purpose and power to work miracles and teach came from His Father.

Are we any different?

Sometimes sleeplessness might mean we need to adjust our diet, our screen time, or our necessary medications. But what if it's our Friend, Jesus, calling out to us, inviting us to be with him? Alone. Together.

I Need a Nap Today

I've made that argument many times. I say things like:

- "I'll be dragging today."

- "I hope I can stay awake at my desk."
- "Bring on the caffeine!"
- "Look at these bags under my eyes!"

But He keeps reminding me of this passage:

"I will restore to you the years that the swarming locust has eaten, the hopper, the destroyer, and the cutter, my great army, which I sent among you. You shall eat in plenty and be satisfied, and praise the name of the Lord your God, who has dealt wondrously with you. And my people shall never again be put to shame." (Joel 2:25-26)

I don't want to make the Bible say something it doesn't say, but the Holy Spirit used this passage to remind me of who God is and what He is capable of doing in my life and yours. He is the God who repays, restores, renews, and refreshes. If He has the power to restore years of devastation and destruction, then He can most certainly restore a few hours of sleep I've lost. And He can give us the strength to get through a long day of physical, mental and emotional challenges even when we're tired or sleep-deprived.

"I can do all things through him who strengthens me." (Phil 4:13)

All things.

He wants us to depend on Him for every need we have, big or small. Whether it's a health crisis, a troubled relationship, or a few hours of lost sleep; He is able to do exceedingly more than we could ask or imagine.

Maybe you should talk to your doctor about why you're having trouble sleeping. But don't neglect to speak to the Great Physician, too. He knows our innermost thoughts, even better than we know them.

Burning the Candle at Both Ends

I'm not suggesting that we should habitually neglect sleep and rest. Rest was God's idea and He even set aside an entire day for us to rest for our good and His glory. But I know I've been guilty of depending on a good night's sleep more than I depend on God who gives me strength.

When God wanted to instruct the boy, Samuel, He called out to Him in the middle of the night. Not recognizing his voice, he thought Eli, the priest, was calling out for him. Finally, Eli realized what was happening and told him this:

> Now Samuel did not yet know the Lord, and the word of the Lord had not yet been revealed to him.
>
> And the Lord called Samuel again the third time. And he arose and went to Eli and said, "Here I am, for you called me." Then Eli perceived that the Lord was calling the boy. Therefore Eli said to Samuel, "Go, lie down, and if he calls you, you shall say, 'Speak, Lord, for your servant hears.'" So Samuel went and lay down in his place. (I Sam 3:7-9)

May I gently suggest: the next time sleeplessness comes, will you consider your need to spend time alone with God and hear what He wants to say to you. He is always ready to meet us when we make time for Him, even in the middle of a long night.

Be with Him.

To know God is our greatest need---even greater than sleep.

Leave your phone. Don't grab the remote. Let the clothes stay unfolded, the dishes unwashed, and the list unmade. Meditate on His Word—a phrase even. "I trust you, Lord" is one of my favorites.

"And those who know your name put their trust in you, for you, O Lord, have not forsaken those who seek you." (Ps 9:10) Repeat it aloud if possible or quietly to yourself. Every thought that comes, reply with "I trust you, Lord." I trust you, Lord, to:

Work it out
Fix it
Heal
Provide
Lead
Comfort
Convict

Leave your life and theirs and all the problems in the world, in His very capable hands and trust Him to repay, restore and renew you for the day ahead. I'll leave you with these verses which remind me of how the Psalmist responded to sleeplessness:

Takeaway Truth

"But his delight is in the law of the LORD, and on His law he meditates day and night." (Ps 1:2)

"By day the Lord commands his steadfast love, and at night his song is with me, a prayer to the God of my life." (Ps 42:8)

"I remember your name in the night, O Lord, and keep your law." (Ps 119:55)

"My eyes are awake before the watches of the night, that I may meditate on your promise." (Ps 119:148)

"My soul waits for the Lord more than watchmen for the morning--more than watchmen waiting for the morning." (Ps 130:6)

"My soul yearns for you in the night; my spirit within me earnestly seeks you." (Isa 26:9)

17

When You House is a Mess

"The wisest woman builds her house, but folly with her own hands tears it down." (Prov 14:1)

I want to be a wise woman who builds her house.

Chapter 14 of Proverbs continues with an admonition to uprightness, and fearing the Lord, and wise lips; just the good stuff you would expect in a book written by the wisest man who ever lived. Then verse 4:

"Where there are no oxen, the manger is clean, but abundant crops come by the strength of the ox." (Proverbs 14:4)

This kind of concrete illustration found throughout the book of Proverbs often seems random and out of place---but nothing in His Word is there by accident. I sensed my lesson today was here, in these 4 verses. I paused and listened. Then I chuckled and thought: where there are no people, the house is clean.

The Oxen in the Manger and Our Messy Homes

I sit for a few moments and meditate on that thought. In this house, there are a lot of dirty dishes, dirty clothes, messy rooms, crumbs on the floor, and spots on the carpet. Usually, the messes are a result of a house full of family and friends who party and fellowship and laugh and cry. The dishes and clothes and rooms and floors get cleaned and stay that way for a moment or a day. But as life is lived messes are made.

- dishes in the sink reflect a meal enjoyed
- dirty clothes smell of sunshine and hard work
- shoes on the living room floor remind me they wanted to stay for a while
- messy rooms reveal a love for books and music and memories
- crumbs on the floor and spots on the carpet echo with conversation and laughter

I get it.

"My manger is messy but my crops are abundant." (Prov 14:4)

There's a time to clean and put away. But I am often guilty of missing the blessing of the messy. When your house is a mess, remember this: *The wisest woman builds her house with gratitude.*

Lord, today I am thankful for the people who inhabit this home. I am thankful for the messes we make. I am thankful for the blessings of life. I am thankful for the lessons in Your Word. I am thankful for You, Lord.

Takeaway Truth

"Give thanks in all circumstances; for this is the will of God in Christ Jesus for you." (I Thess 5:18)

18

When Life Seems All Uphill

There are days when life seems all uphill. You begin the day worn and weary. You start out behind and feel you'll never catch up. The to-do list is longer than any one person can handle and everyone seems to need a piece of you.

I've had my fair share of uphill days. My life isn't all blue skies and get-aways. I've shed a lot of tears in the shower while I plotted my escape. There have many days when I've considered throwing in the towel, giving in and giving up, and sewing a big "L" on my sweater for loser. It's convenient at my age to blame it on hormones, but I've found that this feeling doesn't discriminate. Regardless of age, sex, race or personality type, most of us are going to feel this way at some time or another.

On a recent trip to Cheaha State Park we decided to hike one of our favorite trails. We've hiked this trail many times with our children. We hike down to the lake and get a ride back up the mountain, or we start at the lake and hike up the mountain and back to the campsite. This time we decided to make the hike down and back with a brief water break at the lake. Here's a description of the trail I found.

> This is a rocky hike (or slide if you're not careful) down through a healthy, mixed hardwood/pine forest. But don't gloat for long as you savor the flat walking around Cheaha Lake, because the best part of this hike is the thigh-burning climb back to the top. This hike, which links Cheaha Mountain with Cheaha Lake below, is by far the steepest sustained ascent/descent within Cheaha State Park.[1]

The thigh-burning climb back to the top was all uphill. It was a very steep, sustained ascent. Some of my days have felt that way recently. I learned some things from that hike that have helped me when life seems all uphill.

1. Pace yourself. Some of the hikers started out too fast. The flat part of the trail at the beginning of the ascent is deceiving. Some days are that way, too. We start out too fast, eager to get it all done. If you're in a season when life seems all uphill, slow down. Ease into your day. Step outside and greet the sun. Read a Psalm. Write down five things you're thankful for. Pace yourself.

2. Take a break. As we began the ascent some of the hikers appeared fatigued and winded. They needed to take a break but pressed on to stay ahead. Soon they were forced to take a break or risk heat exhaustion and injury. When life seems all uphill, take a break. Sit down. Look around. Take in the view and listen. Catch your breath and get your second wind. Do it as often as is necessary.

3. Lighten your load. One of the hikers was carrying a bag with water and snacks and first aid supplies. As the ascent grew steeper and legs grew tired, the weight of the bag became almost unbearable to its carrier. Another hiker took over the pack for the remainder of the journey. When life seems all uphill, lighten your load. Ask for help when you need you it. Receive the help that is offered. Let go of an unnecessary burden. Learn to say "no".

4. Refuel. As we neared the top of the mountain one of the hikers said she wasn't feeling well. Knowing this one the way I do I knew her body needed more than water. We insisted she refuel and soon she was feeling much better. When life seems all uphill, make sure you refuel. Listen to your body. Refuel regularly. Have lunch with a friend. Feed yourself well.

5. Look up. We were just a few feet from the end of the trail. I'd hiked it enough to know. But the one who was weary couldn't see it. We were at the steepest part of the trail and the gray boulder walls loomed high, dampening the spirit. I sat down beside her and said, "Look up. The end is right there." She smiled and said, "OK. I can make it." When life seems all uphill, look up. Listen to the One who is always beside you, showing you the way, and walking it with you. Know that there are others on the journey, too. Look up and smile. Breathe in grace and breathe out praise. You can make it.

Takeaway Truth

"Therefore, since we are surrounded by so great a cloud of witnesses, let us also lay aside every weight, and sin which clings so closely, and let us run with endurance the race that is set before us," (Heb 12:1)

19

When You Need Help in the Overwhelm

Overwhelm! We're only a few days into the New Year and I've felt overwhelmed already. I'm not surprised. As a firstborn, Type A, overachiever with a side-order of scatterbrained creativity, I learned how to fight overwhelm before I learned how to drive a car. If you're experiencing overwhelm know that you're not alone. And I want you to know that you can effectively deal with it in a way that doesn't require illegal substances or giving up altogether in a Netflix and chocolate haze. Because I tried the Netflix and chocolate part and it doesn't work.

What is Overwhelm? I doubt I need to define "overwhelm" for you. But just to clarify, here's Webster's definition:

Overwhelm (verb): to bury or drown beneath a huge mass.

Synonyms: swamp, submerge, engulf, bury, flood, inundate

And here's my definition: Overwhelm (noun): the feeling that you'll never get it all done so you might as well quit; the feeling that everyone always needs everything which is more than you could ever give.

Overwhelm is a drama queen.

3 Symptoms of Overwhelm

If you Google "the symptoms of overwhelm" you'll get a long list. But I've noticed three that reoccur most often when I'm feeling overwhelmed:

<u>1. Resentful.</u> When I'm overwhelmed I'm often resentful toward those who seem to be having fun, enjoying life, and succeeding at

their work. My resentment manifests with thoughts and feelings dripping with sarcasm.

"I'm doing all the work!"

"*Somebody* has to worry about it!"

"It must be nice to have plenty of time to relax and play!"

2. Tearful. Feeling overwhelmed also causes me to be unusually tearful. I cry pretty easily (sad stories and church music), but when I'm overwhelmed, I'll cry about anything with anyone. Yes, it's awkward.

3. Forgetful. While occasionally forgetting an appointment or a friend's birthday makes us human, a pattern of forgetfulness, or that frequent nagging feeling that "I'm forgetting something", is often a symptom of being overwhelmed.

3 Causes of Overwhelm

Depending on your circumstances and season of life, the causes of overwhelm may vary; but again, I can almost always trace the general feeling of overwhelm back to these three factors.

1. Doing too much. God never gives us too much to do. We do that to ourselves or allow others to do it to us. I want to do all the things all the time which seems like a pretty great idea until the overwhelm sets in. I've learned my limits, that it's my job to protect my schedule, and that margin is a necessity for peaceful, purposeful living.

2. Failing to plan. Failure to plan and create habits and systems is a recipe for a crisis. When I fail to plan I tend to focus on the urgent rather than the important. And when it comes to what everyone else wants, it's almost always urgent. "I need this done and I need it today!" they say.

Creating habits and systems, having a weekly/monthly/yearly plan allows us to accomplish what we've deemed important. We live purposefully, according to our values and priorities; and, in the event a genuinely urgent matter arises, we are free to choose how we will respond.

3. Going it alone. Asking for help can be hard. I tend to think "I should be able to handle this". But pride is ugly and can drive us deeper into sin by reinforcing an unhealthy self-sufficiency in which we abandon surrender to and dependence upon God. Creator God made us for fellowship. We need Him and we need each other.

The Enemy loves to isolate us. We feel alone and lonely and withdraw instead of reaching up and crying out for help.

3 Healthy Responses to Overwhelm

1. Quit something. I have a hard time saying no when I'm asked to lead, teach, or help with something. But even harder than saying no is saying yes only to realize it was one yes too many. Each time we say yes to something we're saying no to something else. Friends, we can only do so much. There are only so many hours in a day and learning to use those hours for what matters most is an important part of fighting overwhelm. When I'm feeling overwhelmed I know I've probably overcommitted. I find it helpful to sit before the Lord with my commitments and invite Him to show me where and how I've overstepped His plans.

2. Embrace mediocrity. I aspire to excellence in every area of my life. If I'm not careful though, perfectionism replaces excellence and I'm overwhelmed. Excellence inspires. Perfectionism paralyzes. We have to know when to say, "Good enough" and move on.

3. Ask for help. Lastly, we need to know when and how to ask for help. I confess to a stubborn streak when it comes to this but I've discovered a new area of ministry in this season by acknowledging my weaknesses and struggles. I'm encouraged by those who are ahead of me and offer me wisdom and guidance for the journey; and, I've found great joy in encouraging and leading those beside and behind me.

Takeaway Truth

"Fear not, for I am with you; be not dismayed, for I am your God. I will strengthen you, yes, I will help you, I will uphold you with My righteous right hand." (Isa 41:10)

20

When You Think You Need Help

She's just a little girl and she's having trouble. I ask her if she needs help. She replies, "No, I need Hope."

You see, Hope is a person, a young woman to be exact. The little girl lives with Hope and her family and they're our traveling companions this week, as we all enjoy a vacation with friends.

The little girl is attached to Hope. She trusts her like no one else. When she's in need she relies on Hope.

Sometimes I think I need help. Sometimes you probably think I need help. What I really need is hope. Like the little girl, I need help in the form of Hope—the Person—Jesus Christ.

I walk down the hall to find Hope. "She needs you," I tell her. Hope responds. Hope comes to the little girl's rescue.

Our Hope does the same.

We are all, always in desperate need. Our hearts and lips cry for help. Help can be good. But help is temporary. Help is limited. Help is tangible. Help can be bought. What we really need is Hope. Hope always responds. Hope comes to our rescue and gives us the help we need and so much more. Jesus, our Hope, gives us Himself. He is all we need.

Jesus is our only Hope.

Takeaway Truth

"Rejoice in hope." (Rom 12:12)

21

When You Want an Easy Button

Life's been hard lately for me and many of those closest to me and I'm about worn out. Can you relate? "I want an easy button!" If I had $100 for every time I've said that in the last few months, life would be a whole lot easier. Or would it?

An Easy Life

I start my day as usual. Make coffee. Drink a glass of water. Read my Bible and journal what I'm learning. Today's reading is from the books of Isaiah, Micah, and the Gospel of John.

As I read I have more questions than answers. I still don't understand all that I read in God's Word but here's the thing: God speaks even though I don't always fully understand a passage.

I'm sitting in my favorite chair, bare feet resting on the fuzzy stool. Steam rises from a big cup of coffee sitting next to the cold glass of water. I've propped open the back door to listen to the wind blow hard through the trees. I see branches bend and leaves turn loose. The songbirds seem oblivious. A phrase suddenly comes to mind:

Do not pray for an easy life. Pray to be a strong person.

Years ago I had a bulletin board in my kitchen and that anonymous quote hung next to my son's soccer schedule and the card reminding me of a dentist appointment. I haven't thought about in years. Until this morning.

I watch the condensation roll down the glass as I run down the list in my head. I'm overwhelmed by some things and angry about others. I wish life were easier. Why does everything have to be so hard?

"In this world, you will have trouble." (John 16:33, NIV)

Oh yeah.

But I didn't think He meant this. Trouble every day.

Yesterday, I heard a lady say, "I'll be glad when this is over." She paused, smiled, and said, "And then there will be something else." She's a believer. She wasn't being negative or expressing a lack of faith. She was stating a fact.

In this world, you will have trouble. Pray to be a stronger person.

When I was younger, I did. I was full of optimism, determinism, and stick-to-it-ness. I'm older now and I've seen a lot of trouble. I confess that I've let the trouble wear me down. Maybe you have, too.

The Word of God Speaks

God wants to have a word *with us* because He has a word *for us*. Did you get that? Here's what He's saying:

I Am your God

"So do not fear, for I am with you; do not be dismayed, for I am your God. I will strengthen you and help you; I will uphold you with my righteous right hand." (Isa 41:10, NIV)

In this world you will have trouble, remember? We've been reminded by the One Who Knows All Things. He is with us! But not just with us. He has promised to strengthen and help and hold us up!

I Am your strength

"I know how to be brought low, and I know how to abound. In any and every circumstance, I have learned the secret of facing plenty and hunger, abundance and need. I can do all things through him who strengthens me." (Phil 4:12-13)

Even in the midst of trouble, you and I can be content. How? Through Jesus who gives us strength!

I Am your refuge

"God is our refuge and strength, a very present help in trouble. Therefore we will not fear though the earth gives way, though the mountains be moved into the heart of the sea, though its waters roar and foam, though the mountains tremble at its swelling." (Ps 46:1-3)

We're all familiar with the verse, "Be still and know that I am God." It's found in Psalm 46:10, just a few verses after the ones you read above. So take note: "though the earth gives way and the mountains fall into the sea", in other words, when it feels like everything is falling apart, "Be still and know that I am God." How is that even possible? Be still, really? No! We want to do something, anything, to get some relief! How is it even possible that the Psalmist could say "be still"? Because of what he proclaims at the start: "God is our refuge and strength, an ever-present help in trouble." And so we will proclaim with him!

I Am your peace

"Now may the Lord of peace himself give you peace at all times and in every way. The Lord be with all of you." (2 Thess 3:16)

We don't have to have peace around us to have peace within us! Jesus is our peace and He lives in us!

I Am with you

"Be strong and courageous. Do not fear or be in dread of them, for it is the Lord your God who goes with you. He will not leave you or forsake you." (Deut 31:6)

God is with us in every difficult circumstance and trial. We may feel alone but we are never alone!

I Am your help

"But you, O Lord, do not be far off! O you my help, come quickly to my aid!" (Ps 22:19)

I think God is reminding us that His help doesn't always mean He removes our trouble. He's growing our faith through our trouble. As the roots of a tree grow deep and the branches bend without breaking, God is helping us become deeply rooted in Him as our will bends to His.

Pray To Be a Stronger Person

"Do not be anxious about anything, but in every situation, by prayer and petition, with thanksgiving, present your requests to God.

And the peace of God, which transcends all understanding, will guard your hearts and your minds in Christ Jesus." (Phil 4:6-7)

Notice this: present your requests to God . . . and the peace of God. The verse doesn't say, as much as we would like it to, that when we, (1) present our requests, he will (2) grant our requests or fix our problem so that (3) we will have peace. No. It simply says, present your requests to God and you will have peace. Peace doesn't come from the absence of problems but through the presence of Christ!

Peace doesn't come from the absence of problems but through the presence of Christ!

God wants to hear from us! If it concerns us, He wants us to bring it to Him. I wonder what might happen if for a day or a week or a month when we present our requests to God, rather than asking him to fix our problem, zap the difficult people in our life, and just make everything easier, we prayed instead to have greater faith, to trust him more, to shine His light in all the dark places of our lives?

Sure I have troubles and so do you, but we have God with us who has overcome the world and every trouble in it!

So let the wind blow. Our branches will bend to His will and turn loose of ours. And we will sing the song of praise, to the One who has overcome the world!

Takewaway Truth

"I have said these things to you, that in me you may have peace. In the world you will have tribulation. But take heart; I have overcome the world." (John 16:33)

22

When You Want to Run Away

Today is Monday and I want to run away. I am overwhelmed by what I didn't get done last week and by what I need to do this week. I've made lists. I've even made lists of lists. They haunt me. I've organized and decluttered and simplified. Yet, I am overwhelmed.

I sit in the chair in the corner and try to read. Too distracted. I check social media. Too boring. I try to finish the third cup of coffee. Too cold.

I listen to the chatter throughout the house. They talk and laugh and make plans for sleepovers and workouts and swimming. One announces he'll be spending next summer on the west coast and the Rocky Mountains. Really? "How will you be funding that?" I think to myself. I realize I am momentarily resentful of their carefree life and big dreams. "I have real worries," I think to myself. "Like girls going to sleepovers and boys who want to spend the summer on the west coast."

She comes to my room chattering about kittens and brothers, as she lies down on my unmade bed. She notices how soft and cozy and firm it feels. "I love beds like this," she says. I recall nights on the old slip-covered couch because the soft-cozy-firm bed is like concrete to my sleepless self.

"I'm sorry, Mommy, why haven't you ever told me that before." I say nothing. I think of all the things I've never told her. All those Monday morning thoughts and fears that would mar her freckled, carefree life. Too soon she will know. She has a thought and skips out of the room.

I sit in my chair feeling the breeze from the fan. It's hot in here and I don't want to get up. I don't want to do anything, really. My thoughts, unleashed, wander. What can I do that would make me feel better? Eat the home-made ice-cream in the freezer with leftover birthday cake? Where can I run to feel better? The mall? My favorite thrift store? The coffee shop?

Then I hear His Word in my heart.

"Come to me, all who labor and are heavy laden, and I will give you rest." (Matt 11:28)

Oh! How my flesh-walking-self wants to run away and hide and put on the fig leaves that make empty promises. But they only leave me naked—exposed---in the wilderness I've created right in the middle of the paradise He has provided.

The Monday morning feeling has the same cure as the feeling I had so many years ago. Run to Him.

And so I do.

I'm still in my favorite chair in the corner. But I run to Him. I hang up the phone with one speaking of a terminal illness and numbered days and I run to Him. I move clothes from washer to dryer and I run to Him. I look at the calendar and the list and I run to Him.

Takeaway Truth

"Come to me, all who labor and are heavy laden, and I will give you rest." (Matt 11:28)

23

When God Asks Too Much of You

Do you sometimes feel like God is asking too much of you? Like He wants you to do things that are too hard, too big, or too costly in all the ways? Maybe He wants you to do something or maybe He's telling you to wait and do nothing. Is He telling you to take on a new project or let go of a long-held one. Is He asking you to speak up or hold your tongue? Maybe He wants you to crawl out of your hiding place, push through the pain, and go to work. Or maybe He wants you to stop all the busy work and rest. If you're anything like me, then you answered "yes" to several of those questions.

"But I can handle anything!" I often reply. "Perseverance is my superpower."

When the going gets tough I hunker down, make a plan, and get laser-focused. It works every time. God never asks more of me than *I* can handle. At least that's how I tend to see myself. Until He actually asks too much of me.

He's asked me to face unspeakable grief and parenting heartaches; and to rebuild a marriage by His design rather than my own. I've watched dreams die, friends leave, and churches and people fall apart.

And every time God asks too much of me I learn again what God wants most from me.

God is Jehovah-Jireh. He is our Provider. We are introduced to God by this name, Jehovah Jireh—which means The Lord Will Provide---in Genesis 22 when Abraham is about to sacrifice his only son Isaac on Mount Moriah. (I hope you'll go read the story in its entirety!) Every time I think God is asking too much of me, I think of this story.

Side note: Just so you know this is one of those stories in the Bible that's gut-wrenching for me. I won't attempt to try and explain it here but I know for sure God is bigger than what our minds can understand. He says so in His Word!

“For my thoughts are not your thoughts, neither are your ways my ways, declares the Lord. For as the heavens are higher than the earth, so are my ways higher than your ways and my thoughts than your thoughts.” (Isa 55:8-9)

Back to the story:

God provides the lamb for sacrifice and Isaac is spared. It's an amazing story of obedience, surrender, and God's sovereignty that teaches us how to respond when God asks too much of us.

3 Things to Remember When God Asks Too Much of You

1. God is never surprised. He is The All-Knowing, All-Seeing God of Creation. Life comes at us hard and we often feel blindsided by the stuff that happens around us and to us. But God is never surprised or blindsided. He's not scrambling around, wringing his hands, trying to figure out what to do next. Yes, I've often questioned why the all-knowing God would allow certain things to happen---because honestly, life doesn't make sense to me sometimes. But I find comfort in knowing that He knows and I can rest in His wisdom.

2. God has a plan. As we look back on the story of Abraham and Isaac on Mt. Moriah we can see how God had a plan and a purpose all along. He knew when he asked Abraham to offer Isaac as a sacrifice that He would provide the lamb. He also knew that Abraham would obey and we would have a glimpse, even from the Genesis beginning, that God was working His plan to provide Jesus as our sacrificial lamb. Whatever difficult situation you find yourself in, know that God has a plan. He always does. It may not make sense to you and me but the God who created the universe is perfectly capable to act on our behalf.

3. God will provide. He not only has a plan but He is a good, good Father who will act on our behalf according to His wisdom and mercy. In our hard places, we always have a need. Often that need is beyond our ability to provide. God delights in using the

circumstances of our lives to show Himself as our Jehovah-Jireh. He's provided comfort during unspeakable grief, new dreams, new friends and a better-than-before marriage.

He has a provision ready for your greatest need, too.

Why Does God Ask Too Much of You?

I began this post by asking: Do you sometimes feel like God is asking too much of you? If you haven't already come to this conclusion let me make one thing perfectly clear: God asks too much of us because He wants us to know that nothing is too much for Him.

When I feel what He's asking me to do or say or be is too much for me I've learned to see it as a cue to surrender and submit myself to Him once again and let Him be the strength of my life.

Most of us can recite Psalm 46:10, "Be still and know that I am God", but may I remind you how that chapter in Psalms begins? Do you why we can "be still and know"? Because "God is our refuge and strength, a very present help in trouble. Therefore we will not fear though the earth gives way, though the mountains be moved into the heart of the sea, though its waters roar and foam, though the mountains tremble at its swelling.' (Ps 46:1-3)

2 Things You Should Do When God Asks Too Much of You

1. Be the Abraham. From the Scripture, we see that Abraham promptly obeyed what God had instructed him to do.

"So Abraham rose early in the morning, saddled his donkey, and took two of his young men with him, and his son Isaac. And he cut the wood for the burnt offering and arose and went to the place of which God had told him." (Gen 22:3)

No excuses. No waiting. He made use of the resources that had already been provided by God and took the first step in obedience. He obeyed, even to the point of giving up his Isaac, because he trusted God.

2. Be the Isaac. Sometimes the trouble comes from neglecting to obey what God has clearly instructed.

The hard times in life will often require us to lay down our idea of what a job, a relationship, a calling, a life should look like. Isaac was old enough to know something was up.

> And Isaac said to his father Abraham, "My father!"
> And he said, "Here I am, my son."
> He said, "Behold, the fire and the wood, but where is the lamb for a burnt offering?"
> Abraham said, "God will provide for himself the lamb for a burnt offering, my son." So they went both of them together. When they came to the place of which God had told him, Abraham built the altar there and laid the wood in order and bound Isaac his son and laid him on the altar, on top of the wood. (Gen 22:7-9)

There is no evidence that Isaac questioned or resisted. They went, both of them together, obediently, sacrificially, laying down everything for a holy God.

"So here's what I want you to do, God helping you: Take your everyday, ordinary life—your sleeping, eating, going-to-work, and walking-around life—and place it before God as an offering." (Rom 12:1, The Message)

What's too much for you today? Is it a job that hasn't turned out quite how you'd hoped? Are you surprised to find that the one you married has (or hasn't) changed after all these years? Maybe it's a dream you've chased since childhood that dances, always just out of reach. Has God asked you to do, say, or be something that seems impossible?

God is not surprised. He has a plan. He will provide. I've witnessed and experienced it time and again.

I encourage you to take the first step, or continue on, in obedience to God. Gather and use the resources He has so graciously provided. Be willing to lay down your idea, your plan, and your pride on the altar of Providence. God is directing the affairs of each and every one of us for our good and His glory.

Takeaway Truth

"And God is able to make all grace abound to you, so that having all sufficiency in all things at all times, you may abound in every good work." (2 Cor 9:8)

24

When God Shows Up in Your Ordinary Life

I long for greatness---an extraordinary life of eternal significance. Not fame or fortune or celebrity status. Rather the deep need to know that my life matters---that I will leave behind something more than a carbon footprint and a closet full of cute clothes I found at the thrift store.

When God Shows Up In Your Ordinary Life He Calls You To Serve.

This season of life has me folding towels—the same seven towels every single day; and making beds, scrubbing toilets, stirring soup, and teaching math and spelling. Sometimes my life in this loud house on a quiet street in the rural south leaves me with the feeling that somehow it isn't enough---enough for me, enough for them, enough for God. There must be something out there, over there, bigger and better than this.

"Again, the devil took him to a very high mountain and showed him all the kingdoms of the world and their glory. And he said to him, 'All these I will give you, if you will fall down and worship me.'" (Matt 4: 8-9)

Whatever our job or our role, we can spend our hours and our days constructing grand plans and elaborate schemes. Dreaming of our escape from this day of doing the thing we've done a hundred times before or every day for weeks, or years or decades. We begin our days with dread and end them with regret. We loathe the same-old-same-old and regret that we lived another day walking down the same street and falling into the same hole.

When someone asks, “How was your day?” we reply, “Good” or “Busy” or “Long”.

Why do we never reply, "Extraordinary!"? Is not every minute sacred? Is not every breath a gift from God? Is not every task done before a holy master?

“Then Jesus said to him, ‘Be gone, Satan! For it is written, You shall worship the Lord your God and him only shall you serve.’” (Matt 4:10)

I am learning. Jesus is my teacher. God chooses the simple and makes it sacred. He teaches me how to make the ordinary extraordinary. How to turn water into wine.

When God Shows Up In Your Ordinary Life He Calls You To The Cross.

My Enemy shows me the kingdoms of this world and tempts me with self-worship. My Savior shows me the cross and calls me to die to myself.

In my ordinary life I scrub a 1960’s-Harvest-Gold-non-self-cleaning-oven; He teaches me that no amount of scrubbing will make me clean. Only He can do that.

I clean clutter from a closet; He reveals clutter in my heart; souvenirs of unpleasant experiences and painful memories. He invites me to give them to Him.

I lie in bed, eyes wide open, sleepless with thoughts of unfinished tasks and tomorrow's new list. He reminds me that He always finishes what He starts and that includes me.

I am learning that in Him I am clean, uncluttered, and complete.

When God Shows Up In Your Ordinary Life He Calls You To Live For Him.

With Him, my ordinary life is quite extraordinary. Eternally significant. A task of heavenly proportion.

“Then the Devil left Him, and immediately angels came and began to serve Him.” (Matt 4:11)

Takeaway Truth

"Many are the plans in the mind of a man, but it is the purpose of the Lord that will stand." (Prov 19:21)

25

When Ironing is Holy Work

She lifts the ironing board from the hooks on the back of the laundry room door. There's just enough floor space between the laundry baskets and the litter box to set up her work station. The ironing board could use some WD-40 but the finger-nails-on-a-chalkboard-screeching-sound it makes as she opens it, is a welcome prelude to the worship and work that's ahead. She raises a hand and reaches overhead for the inexpensive, but dependable iron. The water in the reservoir gurgles signaling that it's time to lay it down.

Ironing is Holy Work

She lays down shirts and pants wrinkled after a good cleaning. Collars and sleeves, pockets and cuffs get pressed one by one. She lays down confession and praise, too. Pressing through questions without answers, hoping, praying, and waiting to hear Him before the job is done.

Her circumstances in this moment are not random. He orchestrated every detail.

As a teenager, someone else did the ironing. As a twenty-something-student-wife she didn't buy what required ironing or they wore it wrinkled. The grown-up thirties racked regular trips to the cleaners and requests for extra-starch. (Thank you, 1992.) During all those years she followed His call with reckless abandon.

Today is no different.

Because she's learned that having a resume of what's she's accomplished is less important than who she's becoming. Because she's learning to see every situation in which she finds herself as the means of obtaining a greater knowledge of Jesus Christ.

So she follows His call with reckless abandon in total surrender to him. And ironing becomes holy work.

The Holy Spirit is determined that we will have the realization of Jesus Christ in every area of our lives, and He will bring us back to the same point over and over again until we do.

The point he brings her back to is this:

> Whatever we may be doing— even eating, drinking, washing disciples' feet, [or ironing] — we have to take the initiative of realizing and recognizing Jesus Christ in it. Every phase of our life has its counterpart in the life of Jesus. Our Lord realized His relationship to the Father even in the most menial task. "Jesus, knowing…that He had come from God and was going to God…took a towel…and began to wash the disciples feet…" (John 13:3-5).[1]

Your Reckless Abandon

Have you yet realized your relationship with God in your most menial tasks? All our work becomes holy work when we recognize Jesus in it. Your faithfulness in the ordinary---even unpleasant---things of life is an opportunity to be like Christ, teaching and demonstrating God's ways, to the world around you.

"Christ says, 'Give me All. I don't want so much of your time and so much of your money and so much of your work: I want You.'"[2]

Takeaway Truth

"Humble yourselves before the Lord, and he will exalt you." (James 4:10)

26

When Ordinary Life Feels Overwhelming

Today is an ordinary day. Most of my days have been ordinary days. Maybe your days feel that way, too. See if this sounds familiar?

We get up, drink coffee and eat the same thing for breakfast. We wear the same outfit over and over (no matter how many clothes we own) because it fits and is comfortable. We make our bed, check social media, and brush our teeth. We eat lunch with the same people in the same place or alone. Again. We care for children, grandchildren, our spouse or elderly parents.

I could go on but you get the idea. We do the same things day after day, year after year. We daydream of the next vacation or shopping trip or holiday or try to hold on until the weekend.

The enemy convinces us that "surely there's more to life than this", or "maybe you missed your purpose", or "the grass is greener somewhere else". Don't listen to him. He's a liar and he's always, always lying.

Listen to Jesus! Jesus is here---in the ordinary. And He is anything but ordinary. He has come that you and I might have the abundant life-- our ordinary life made abundant through Him. He is extraordinary in the ordinary. Look for Him.

He's in the laundry room and the conference room. He's at the breakfast table and the business lunch. He's in the home-school and the public school. He's everywhere. Look for Him.

"You will seek me and find me when you seek me with all your heart. I will be found by you, declares the Lord." (Jer 29:13-14)

When your ordinary life feels overwhelming remember this:

1. Jesus wants you to know He's with you. He's not a ghostly stalker hiding out of sight, trying not to be seen. He tells us in His word, "I am with you always," and we can see Him if we'll look.

2. Jesus wants you to depend on Him. Your boss might want you to be an independent self-starter who takes the initiative to solve problems. Jesus wants you to acknowledge your weakness, helplessness, and depend on Him.

I'm reminded of a few times where Jesus was helpful to people engaged in ordinary tasks:

- a woman drawing water at a well (John 4)
- a woman frustrated by kitchen duty during Bible study (Luke 10:38-42)
- a party planner upset about running out of beverages (John 2:1-11)
- a parent with a sick child (Mark 5:21-43)

We want to see miracles and live! The good news is that we're not tasked with doing miracles! That's God's job and He's a genius miracle worker!

Our job is to invite Him into our ordinary days and let Him be God. If there's something more He wants us to do, a change He wants us to make, or a move to greener pastures He has planned, He'll tell us, give us what we need to get there, and walk with us to it and through it!

Sometimes He also might need for us to:

- get out of the way with our overthinking, overanalyzing, and incessant worrying
- stop trying to fix everything and everybody
- talk less and listen more
- work harder
- get out of our comfort zone
- celebrate with someone who's happy
- cry with someone who's grieving

I don't know exactly what you're supposed to do today but God does! Read His Word, ask Him questions, listen for His answer, and then get busy doing what He's told you to do (even if it's just the next small step)!

Takeaway Truth

"For we are his workmanship, created in Christ Jesus for good works, which God prepared beforehand, that we should walk in them." (Eph 2:10)

27

When You Have to Sell Mama and Daddy's Stuff

One of these days, if I die before Jesus comes back, all of my dearly beloved thrift store finds will find their way back to the thrift store or sold cheap at a yard sale. I kind of hate I'll miss it. Not really. I do love a good yard sale, but Jesus is my treasure! He really is.

There's nothing quite like sorting through the contents of someone's home and life to make you take stock of how you want to live and die. Since our marriage in 1987, we've said goodbye to all of our grandparents and our parents. I really didn't expect to be the matriarch of the family at fifty but here I am in skinny jeans and flip flops trying to sort it out.

Speaking of yard sales, my sister and I had a big one this past weekend at my mom and dad's house. We've spent weeks sorting through what we'd keep and what needed to find a new home. It's not an easy task. Many of you reading this have been through it and a few of you are dreading it. I'd like to share what I've learned.

What I've Learned about Sorting and Selling Mamma and Daddy's Stuff

1. There will be tears. Lots and lots of tears. They'll come when you least expect it and often at the most inconvenient times about the smallest things. Let them come. Don't apologize. Don't try to explain. Those who've been there will understand and be okay and those who've yet to be there will not understand and you can't make them. Bear with them.

2. There will be laughter. Lots and lots of laughter. You'll laugh when you least expect it and often at the most inappropriate time. Laugh anyway. Laugh till you cry. Don't apologize. Don't feel ashamed. Laughter is good medicine. Again, those who've been there will understand and be okay and those who've yet to be there won't and you can't make them.

3. There will be guilt. Lots of it at times. Mamma and daddy loved their home and worked hard over many years to make it a beautiful, inviting place to raise a family and serve others. And while it served its purpose during every moment of their lives, their home and all of their things are not meant to serve the same purpose in our lives. We honor them by remembering their life, acknowledging their legacy, and letting go of the guilt that would hinder living the life God has purposed for us.

4. There will be judgment and criticism. Lots of it at times. It'll be passed out with a smile and hug when you least expect, by those you least expect, which makes it hurt even more. Let it fall. Let the judgmental words and shaming opinions and two-cents-worth suggestions fall right in front of you where and when they're spoken. Don't receive them. Don't go back and pick them up later and dissect them. And for goodness sake, don't pass them along. Silence is golden at times like this. Awkward? Maybe. But I've found it's the best way to deal with those people who want to point out that the grass needs cutting, and the grave needs flowers, and the house and everything in it should be enshrined forever. This brings me to my final thought.

There will be one thing you can't sort and sell. Memories. No matter how hard you try you can't sort a memory. Like tears and laughter, memories come when you least expect them. They can be triggered by the words of a song or a scent from the kitchen. Embrace the good ones. Let the painful ones fade. And remember that you certainly can't sell them.

- I can sell daddy's old boots but not the miles we walked together in the woods.
- I can sell daddy's beloved hound dogs but not the howls that echo through the hollow.
- I can sell mamma's dishes but not the thousands of meals prepared with love.

- I can sell mamma's sewing machine but not the hours I watched her measure, cut and stitch.
- I can sell their camper but not the joy and laughter around a crackling camp fire.

As old friends and acquaintances came by their house for the yard sale, we were reminded that the stuff we sorted on racks and tables wasn't mamma and daddy's treasure. Their real treasure and our inheritance is Jesus. For hours we laughed and cried and reminisced. It was a good day. Even in their death they're impacting how we live. In their absence, we march on in faith, hard work, and sweet fellowship because our hope is in the Lord.

One day I'll leave this world and all my kids will be fightin' over who gets the good junk. Not really. I've made them promise they'll just bag it all up and haul it to the thrift store and have a pizza party to celebrate. 'Cause you can't sort and sell the memories if you wanted to you and a yard sale would hardly be worth the trouble. But mostly because I pray that Jesus will always be their greatest treasure.

Takeaway Truth

"When the perishable puts on the imperishable, and the mortal puts on immortality, then shall come to pass the saying that is written: "Death is swallowed up in victory. O death, where is your victory? O death, where is your sting?" The sting of death is sin, and the power of sin is the law. But thanks be to God, who gives us the victory through our Lord Jesus Christ. Therefore, my beloved brothers, be steadfast, immovable, always abounding in the work of the Lord, knowing that in the Lord your labor is not in vain." (I Cor 15:54-58)

28

When You're Not Doing What You Love

Are you doing what you love? I hope you are! But if your life is anything like mine you may find yourself, at some point, not doing what you love. I've had lots of jobs I didn't love to do and even now have to do certain tasks that I don't love doing.

Sometimes no matter how hard we work, or how much we learn, or how we persevere in pursuit of a life we love, we find ourselves in some difficult places. Most of the time we hang on, have faith and keep going.

But I'm concerned about a dangerous message being preached in our culture that says you're wasting your time if you're not doing what you love.

Making Bricks

The children of Israel were there, in Egypt, for over four hundred years. In Genesis 15:13, the Lord tells Abraham, "Know for certain that your offspring will be sojourners in a land that is not theirs and will be servants there, and they will be afflicted for four hundred years." God knew it would happen, and He revealed part of the plan to Abraham.

They were in a place not doing what they loved, seemingly wasting their time making bricks and building cities to satisfy Pharaoh's dream. And God was with them.

Are you wasting your time?

The world says you're wasting your time if you're not doing what you love.

Really?

We can choose the positive spin and see this as a motivational mantra encouraging us to pursue a life of purpose and passion. But it's an incomplete assessment of the life we've been called to live as Christ followers.

The abundant life is not about doing what you love, but loving God in all you do.

Perspective is the key.

If you don't love what you do---the job or tasks required of you---but you do it in the presence and power of God, you're not wasting your time. Time with God is never wasted time. Friend, God is with you. He is always with you.

Are you in a job or career you don't love? A relationship you don't love? A city you don't love? A situation you don't love? God is there. God. Is. There. Be with Him. Be still in the midst of unlovely days and know that He is God.

"Trust in the Lord, and do good; dwell in the land and befriend faithfulness. Delight yourself in the Lord, and he will give you the desires of your heart." (Ps 37:3-4)

The Lord provided a deliverer for Israel according to His plan and purposes. He has a plan and purpose for your life, too. He is working His holy purpose and nothing is wasted. Trust in the Lord. Wait for Him.

Takeaway Truth

"Being strengthened with all power, according to his glorious might, for all endurance and patience with joy;" (Col 1:11)

29

When You Wake Up Crying

I wake up crying. Tears streaming, heart heavy. I lie there for a moment collecting my thoughts, happy that he is already up to make the coffee. I don't want to have to explain or talk about my grief.

Grief is like a weird friend. She shows up uninvited and usually at the most inconvenient times. She's that practical joker that hides behind a tree or around a corner and jumps out when you walk by. You jump startled, your heart races as she laughs at your surprise and horror once again. Anger mixed with embarrassment is what I feel after she blindsides me for the umpteenth time.

And today I'm crying before I've had my first cup of coffee. To wake up crying is not the best way to start your day.

In my dream I was at an outdoor flea market. No surprise there, huh? Flea markets are my happy place. I stroll from one booth to the next when something catches my eye. I think to call daddy and ask him if he needs it or wants it or even if it's a good price. And then I remember. I can't call him. He's not here anymore.

I walk on through the flea market trying to distract my heart with doodads and iron sculptures and t-shirts. I can't hold it in. Tears come. Right there in the middle of it all I stand on a dusty road and weep.

And I awake. Weeping.

Grief's Gift

We meet each other in the hallway at church or the grocery store and exchange pleasantries. You say, "I've been thinking about you" and then ask how I'm doing. I almost always say, "Great!" because at that moment I am. Really. And because it never feels like the right time to tell you about how I woke up crying after I had a dream about being at a flea market and remembering that my dad had died. Even typing those words feels hard and awkward.

Our grief stories cannot be told completely. What I mean is that there are no adequate words in our spoken language to express the complexity of what we feel when we lose someone. So often when I share my sadness over a loss with you I'm left feeling silly about what I've said or sad that I left so much unsaid.

Typing these words on this page is my gift to you, my grieving friend, and to me.

Every human knows grief. We all know what it feels like to wake up crying, to cry in the shower, or at the mall, or while driving in a car alone after a memory or a song or a scent hits our heart like a sledge hammer. It may be the grief of this year's loss or from ten years ago. Either way we almost never see it coming. I write this to simply say, "Me, too."

Grief Without Regret

I'm feeling a bit of a grief hangover from my dream---heavy heart, vague sadness, and slightly puffy, red eyes. But there's no place for regret in grief. No regret that we love. No regret that we dream and remember. No regret that we grieve. And yet, grief isn't a place we live any more than I live in my dream.

So I write my words and dry my tears and make coffee. I do laundry and take a shower. I face this day and my life thankful. I am thankful that I have so much to love and so much to lose. I am thankful that there's so much more to life than loss. I am thankful that my grief has an expiration date because of Jesus.

So let us weep when sadness comes. And then, let us live.

Takeaway Truth

"The LORD is close to the brokenhearted and saves those who are crushed in spirit." (Ps 34:18)

30

When Mother-Love Becomes Idol-Worship

My children aren't the first idols to occupy space on the shelf of my heart; but there is a very special spot reserved for them. Each one can command my mind's attention and my heart's affection like nothing else. That's the definition of worship you know? The mind's attention and the heart's affection set on the object to be adored.

While I might refer to my children as adorable, they are not to be worshipped. God's Word is clear that God alone is to be the object of our worship. But oh how often I allow other things---good things even---like my children, to take the place of the One who made me and saved me.

When God commanded Abraham to offer his son, Isaac, as a sacrifice on Mount Moriah, Abraham obeyed. If we step back from this familiar, heartbreaking scene we can see that his obedience was swift and steady even in the wake of family drama and personal crisis brought about by his own sinful choices.

Remember:

- He passed his lovely wife off as his sister (twice!) out of fear for his own safety in a foreign land.
- He and Sarah were childless and had taken matters into their own hands despite being promised a son by God.

The result of this disobedience was great heartache for the women, the children, and, no doubt, the friends and family who knew and loved them.

But God was always at work perfecting His purpose. In each act of disobedience God was present—chastising, forgiving, redeeming, and renewing what Abraham had tarnished. As Hagar, Sara's maid, prepared to die in the wilderness along with Abraham's son Ishmael, God intervened.

"She gave this name to the LORD who spoke to her: 'You are the God who sees me,' for she said, 'I have now seen the One who sees me.'" (Gen 16:13 NIV)

And then:

"When Abram was ninety-nine years old, the LORD appeared to him and said, 'I am God Almighty; walk before me faithfully and be blameless. I will establish My covenant between Me and you, and I will multiply you exceedingly.'" (Gen 17:1-2 NIV)

No doubt Abraham's history with the All-Sufficient One Who Sees came to bear when God asked him to provide his son, his only son whom he loved, as a sacrifice.

He chose obedience. God wants us to do the same. He is at work in our lives as mothers, perfecting His purpose in us and through us to the ones we love.

We must be willing to tear down the idolatrous high places that seduce us away from our worship of the One True God and lay on the altar of sacrifice anything that would come between our heart and His.

Nothing can hold a candle to the captivating love a mother has for her children. Love is good. Worship and devotion are not. Love for our children should not displace or overshadow the love we have for God and the commitment He requires in our service to Him.

God never intended for Isaac to die. He condemned child sacrifice, a practice of pagan religions, in Leviticus 18:21 and 20:1. God only wanted to kill anything that took His rightful place in Abraham's heart. Abraham's testing taught him what God already knew. When we give God first place in our heart He will provide all that we need and give to us far more than we could ever sacrifice.

As mothers there is much more at stake here than simply our own heart. With every breath we impart the lessons of life to our children. Certainly more than any other skill we want to teach or quality we want to instill, devotion to the One True God is above all else.

Having him as first place in our heart will lead them to keep Him as first place in theirs. All other loves — husband, children, grandchildren — will find their rightful place in our life and know a love from us that is pure and undefiled when God is on the throne of our life.

Six Questions Every Mother Needs to Ask (Regardless of how old your children are.)

1. Do I love my children more than I love God?
2. Are my commitments of time, energy, and resources to my children out of love and obedience to God or a result of the worship of my children and adoration of self?
3. Do they know that their sweet lives are dear to me but not more so than my life in Christ?
4. Have they learned that I can be seduced into discontentment and disobedience by peer pressure?
5. Can they sense that a carefully timed whine or pout will weaken my resolve to be obedient to my God-given task?
6. Would they say that nothing occupies the throne of my heart but God?

God has entrusted our children to us to be nurtured and loved. But our most important task is to point them to Him.

God sees and knows all that you need. He is your All-Sufficient One. Give God first place in your heart and entrust your children to Him.

Takeaway Truth

"Thus says the Lord: 'Let not the wise man boast in his wisdom, let not the mighty man boast in his might, let not the rich man boast in his riches, but let him who boasts boast in this, that he understands and knows me, that I am the Lord who practices steadfast love, justice, and righteousness in the earth. For in these things I delight, declares the Lord.'" (Jer 9:23-24)

31

When You've Been Insulted

The world offers many suggestions for how to handle an insult. I've tried a few only to find I've made a painful experience worse. Life is hard enough without self-inflicted pain.

The Insult

I thought after years of homeschooling the insults wouldn't sting as much. And when they're hurled at me they didn't. Because not only do I not regret homeschooling, I praise God that He lead me in that direction. It's been a blessing to my family and me. But when those insults were hurled directly at my kids—do I even have to explain how that made me feel? Surely, every parent can understand whether it's about homeschooling or something else.

When they came home and told me the story (I'll spare you the painful details), my first question was, "So what did you say?" Their response: "I said thank you because at the end he wished me good luck in life 'under the circumstances'".

My kids shared these stories with me and laughed about them. I wasn't laughing. Mammas have a desire to protect no matter the ages of their children. But my children didn't need protecting. They already knew what the Spirit was about to teach me—again.

The Aftermath

I gave my thoughts and feelings to the Lord instead of doing all the things I wanted to do. That's when I read this verse in my Bible Reading Plan.

"The prudent overlook an insult." (Prov 12: 16)

The Spirit touched my heart immediately and said, "Let it go, Stacy."

I studied the verse a bit to be sure I fully understood it's meaning and learned that God's Word gives us at least four different ways to deal with an insult, just in this one verse! The Hebrew word for "overlooks" can be translated several different ways and each one gives us an option for dealing with an insult.

How to Handle an Insult

1. Overlook it. Like when you're trying to find your keys and you can't, even though they're lying in plain sight. We overlook our keys because there are so many places to look and so much to look at. Do this with an insult. When it happens or you're reminded of it, overlook it by choosing to look somewhere else at something else. Change your focus.

2. Quietly shrug it off. My mom was so good at this. When someone said an unkind word to her or life didn't go her way she would literally shrug her shoulders and say, "Oh, well." I'm learning to do that. It's amazing how freeing it is to just "shrug it off". Try it right now. Just shrug your shoulders and say, "Oh, well." Don't you feel better already?

3. Stay calm. One of my kids admitted going into another room at work after the insult occurred and praying about it. She said she could feel herself getting angry and didn't want to lose her temper or allow it to affect her work. Prayer is the best way I know to stay calm. Remember: Jesus is right where you are, hearing what you hear, feeling what you feel. Talk to him about it and invite him to help you stay calm.

4. Ignore it. I'm not saying ignore the person. One of my kids explained how he stayed engaged with the person but just let his words "fall to the ground". They fell and he chose not to pick them up. Words are heavy, you know? When someone insults you, ignore it. You can choose not to catch the words they toss your way. Picture their words just falling to the ground in front of you. If you're carrying around heavy words someone spoke to you this week or ten years ago, drop them right where you are. Watch them fall and feel the weight that's been lifted.

Why We Should Respond This Way

1. By definition, an insult is meant to offend. An offense is a bait Satan uses to enslave us in the trap of our own ego. The potential to be offended is always present especially when we are insulted. Avoid the bait and respond in wisdom.

2. It's no time to argue and debate. A person shooting fiery arrows probably isn't interested in having a meaningful conversation.

3. Perhaps the person making the remarks is having a bad day and will later regret their words. We have the opportunity to keep our peace and offer it to them.

4. Most importantly, the Bible instructs us to respond this way and Christ modeled it.

Earlier this week I read this:

"It was good for me to be afflicted so I might learn your decrees." (Ps 119: 71)

I'm glad I had the opportunity to be insulted or feel the insults hurled at my children. It provided an opportunity for me to surrender my ways to God, receive grace, and learn a better way.

Takeaway Truth

"The prudent overlook an insult." (Prov 12: 16)

32

When You're Not Enough

"You are enough." I wish the internet would stop telling me that because I'm not. I'm not enough. Repeating those three words—I am enough—over and over or wearing a cute t-shirt with the phrase, won't make it so any more than wearing a Marvel t-shirt will make me a superhero.

I know the saying's been around for a while and lots of people have weighed in on both sides. But it's dangerous self-help garbage in my opinion. If you're reading this thinking, "Lighten up, woman!" it's okay. I've been told that before. Lots of times.

When I was a teenager, I would "argue the horns off a Billy goat" just for the sake of arguing. And I always had to have the last word. Over the last few decades, I've learned to pick my battles and keep my mouth shut about stuff that doesn't matter.

But this matters.

Running On Empty

My gas light is on and I press the display button to see the range-in-miles my car's computer says I have left. "I'm pretty sure I can make it to the gas station near my house," I think to myself opting not to stop at the three gas stations I pass along the way. I'm even tempted to pass the last one and wait until morning to get gas but I hear my daddy's voice in my head saying, "What if you have an emergency in the middle of the night and you don't have any gas in the car." (I've had to stop in the middle of a minor emergency to get gas before. Not fun.)

So I pull into the station and fill up.

When my kids were young and all at home, I tried to never let my gas-guzzling SUV dip below a quarter of a tank. I knew I could get just about anywhere I needed to be with that much fuel. Now that I'm in a different season of life I've downsized to a more fuel-friendly car and I find myself becoming more careless. A lot of days I'm running on empty, trusting the accuracy of a man-made sensor, and relying on my own calculations.

A lot of us are doing the same thing in life.

Until we are willing to accept we are not enough, we'll never be able to accept how desperately we need Jesus to help us put one foot in front of the other. We'll always be calculating exactly how much farther we can go on the gas in our tank.

I Am Not Enough

I am not enough and neither are you. We are all sinners in need of the saving work of Jesus Christ. We cannot save ourselves. Furthermore, once we're saved, we can't live the Christian life without constantly surrendering to the Holy Spirit's ever-present help. Parenting, wife-ing, homemaking, serving, teaching, managing, friending, cleaning, cooking, driving, planning.

No matter how hard we try to be enough or tell ourselves we're enough, we'll always fall short. We are not enough. In our own strength we are destined to live in a constant state of overwhelm, anxious thoughts, and feelings of failure. We'll look for ways to drown our sorrows or run away.

But just like all those gas stations I drive by numerous times a day, resisting, denying the readily available fuel that will fill my tank, we resist and deny the emptiness of our souls, stubbornly calculating how much farther we think we can go on our own.

So Why Do We Do It?

Why do we insist on allowing---forcing even---our souls to run on empty? The answer is simple. Sin.

We are sinners. Hard-headed, prideful, humans determined to do it our way. Even though that statement alone proves that we are not enough, we continue to believe the lie of the Enemy that says, "You're tough. You're strong. You've got what it takes! You're enough! Do better and try a little harder. One. More. Time." We hear

"One. More. Time." and think this time will be it. I can white-knuckle my way through it one. more. time.

I often share that perseverance is my superpower. But it's also my kryptonite. Self-sufficiency, resourcefulness, stick-to-it-ability are admirable character traits but they must not be mistaken for a power source.

What's The Solution?

Surrender. Admit that you are not enough. Say it right now; aloud if possible, "I am not enough." And then take a long deep breath. Inhale grace and exhale peace knowing that you are not enough and it's okay. Rest your weakness in the strong hands of the Father who wants you to surrender and be completely dependent on His strength.

"For the sake of Christ, then, I am content with weaknesses, insults, hardships, persecutions, and calamities. For when I am weak, then I am strong." (2 Cor 12:10)

I'm not okay and you're not okay and it's okay!

God never tells us to be enough. Over and again in His Word, He tells us that He is enough. He tells us to "Come to me, all who labor and are heavy laden, and I will give you rest." (Matt 11:28)

In *Die Young*, Hayley Dimarco says, "As our faith grows and we come to know more about the attributes of God and his role in our lives and our obedience, we learn to see our weakness in light of these words: 'For it is God who works in you, both to will and to work for his good pleasure" (Phil 2:13). And this is where weakness turns into strength, where we go from feeble self-driven soul to strong Spirit-led believer.'"[1]

We can rely on the accuracy of our car's fuel gauge and our own calculations to tell us how much farther our tank of fuel will carry us. The worst that can happen is that we run out of gas on the side of the road and phone a friend for help. But there's much more at stake where our souls are concerned.

I love what Aimee Joseph said in her article ***Enough with 'I am enough'***:

> I reject the phrase "I am enough," not because I don't believe that people who say it mean well, but because God's

> solution to the human dilemma is far better than a platitude. Even if it is harder to swallow at first.[2]

The good news is that we have a Creator who is profoundly interested in the condition of our souls. He knows us better than we know ourselves. He knows exactly what we need, when we need it, and is willing and able to provide according to His riches.

Remember this:

1. I am not enough and you are not enough and it's okay. "The righteousness of God through faith in Jesus Christ for all who believe. For there is no distinction: for all have sinned and fall short of the glory of God." (Rom 3:22-23)

2. God is enough. He has more than enough of whatever you need. "And God is able to make all grace abound to you, so that having all sufficiency in all things at all times, you may abound in every good work." (2 Cor 9:8)

3. He is near. Child of God, He's not waiting for you to get it together before He acts on your behalf. "But God shows his love for us in that while we were still sinners, Christ died for us." (Rom 5:8)

4. Lord, help me. Stop using this as a mindless phrase and make it your prayer every time you feel overwhelmed. "Fear not, for I am with you; be not dismayed, for I am your God; I will strengthen you, I will help you, I will uphold you with my righteous right hand." (Isa 41:10)

5. Pass it along. Give the overwhelmed family and friends around you permission to not be enough. Share your struggle (briefly) and tell them: a) it's okay to be human, b) because God is God, and c) He is near.

Takeaway Truth:

"For the sake of Christ, then, I am content with weaknesses, insults, hardships, persecutions, and calamities. For when I am weak, then I am strong." (2 Cor 12:10)

33

When You Need to Hear God Say "I Love You"

For most of my life my priorities looked something like this: God first, others second ("others" is a long list), and myself last. To have it any other way felt selfish and unchristian. But my noble attempt to live like Jesus turned into an unholy, self-loathing God never intended. He's teaching me a better way.

"Momma, Are You Mad?"

My priorities were all wrong and as I look back over the last two decades I can see what it's cost me. At times, bitterness, resentment, jealousy, and frustration were brewing just below the surface of my inner life. I was sure I was hiding it well. I was wrong.

"Momma, are you mad?" I've been asked that question a few times throughout my mothering years. It pains me now to remember.

"What makes you think I'm mad?" I would say, slightly irritated by the question.

"You just look like you're mad."

"Well, I've just got a lot on my mind," I'd respond in my "you-don't-have-a-clue-how-hard-it-is-to-be-an-adult" tone. Somehow I felt justified to look mad or worried or tired or whatever negative emotion I was feeling.

I want to be careful not to oversimplify the issue here. There are times when we are grieving or experiencing emotional or physical pain and our face shows it. That's okay. And it's okay to share appropriately with our children or close friends how or why we're hurting.

But what I'm really addressing here is the long face we're in the habit of wearing.

We're quick to accuse others of taking advantage of us or not helping enough or not realizing how hard our life is, but oftentimes we're really angry at ourselves and shifting blame to others. That way of living is anything but the abundant life.

Sally Clarkson, in her book, *Own Your Life: Living with Deep Intention, Bold Faith, and Generous Love* says, "Christian means 'Christ in one.' When we live in Him, we are 'in Christ Jesus.' When I learned this secret —owning the Holy Spirit's strength in my life—I was transformed. Christians cannot flourish apart from making God's Spirit the source of their spiritual lives".[1]

What great love the father has lavished on us!

I want to share two specific ways God has intimately revealed how much he loves me as his beloved child.

I was standing in a worship service praying specifically for two friends. As I was praying, I imagined myself walking toward Jesus with these two friends on either side of me. As we approached, I pressed them *toward Him* and I took a step back. Immediately, Jesus reached past them and took hold of me and embraced me. He spoke to me, "I love you, too, Stacy. I care about you and your life. You are precious to me." I began to weep. I really wanted to sob out loud in church. Gasp! (When was the last time you heard anyone sob out loud in church? I remember a story about a woman who wept bitterly. The priest accused her of being drunk.) (I Sam 1:12-14) So I restrained my weeping and He continued to speak to me about my need to pray for myself. To be open about what I'm feeling. To ask for what I need and want. To love myself because He loves me so much.

2. Just before I was to leave on a mission trip to Africa, I was in a room where several small groups of people had gathered to pray. I first heard my name spoken aloud in the group I was in and then several more times in the small groups that were near me. The groups were all praying at once and to most, it probably sounded like unintelligible mumbling. But I believe the Lord allowed me to hear my name being spoken to Him in prayer to calm my anxious heart about a need in my life. I felt His peace and comfort and

sensed Him saying, "I love you. I'm holding you and I'll give you what you need."

During this season of my life, He is teaching me the importance of self-care and how to rearrange my priorities in a God-honoring way that leads to the abundant life He offers. God loves you as His beloved son or daughter and I believe He wants me to share with you what I've learned and trust that you will apply it appropriately to the season you're in.

Me First!

We're all familiar with the instruction to "put your oxygen mask on first before assisting others" (even your own child). That's a life or death decision at 39,000 feet and not at all selfish. If you're incapacitated you'll certainly be no help to anyone around you. The same is true in life.

With God's help, we can learn what it means to live and love and work the way Jesus did to the glory of God.

Together let us echo Sally Clarkson's sentiment: "I do hope that the older I get, the more it can be said of me, "She walks with God. You can see Him in the way she lives, the words she speaks, the peace and humility she has about her, and the way she depends on Him. When you are with her, you feel like you have been with Him."

Takeaway Truth

"See what kind of love the Father has given to us, that we should be called children of God; and so we are. The reason why the world does not know us is that it did not know him." (I John 3:1)

34

When You Don't Know What to Do With Your Life

Delight yourself in the Lord; and he will give you the desires of your heart. (Ps 37:4)

I've had some trouble with that verse over the years. It's a love-hate relationship with fifteen words, really. So I want to tell you a story that might explain how I've come to terms with this promise from God's Word and how you can, too.

I have one sibling, a sister, who's almost three years younger than me. She's been my hairstylist since we were teens. We've lived and loved through perms, big hair, side ponytails, all the braids, crimping, flatirons, and enhancing my gray strands. I trust her implicitly. I've driven miles and miles to sit in her chair so she can work her magic. She's a gifted stylist and owns a beautiful salon. Those hair appointments are also a good excuse for us to talk and laugh and stay connected.

Each time I sit down in her chair she asks, "So what are we doing today?"

For almost thirty years, my response has been the same: "I have no idea. What do you think I need?" She'll ask a few questions and off she goes to mix her magic potions.

I can confidently ask her the question—what do you think I need— and trust her with an outcome I love because she's an expert, she knows me and my heart, she loves me, and she wants what's best for me. I always love my hair! Our system works!

As I reflect on my life, I realize the same system works there, too. But I must take care to adhere to the conditions if I want the promised outcome.

"Commit your way to the Lord; trust in him, and he will act." (Ps 37:5)

When I sit in the expert hairstylist's chair I'm committed to her—I trust her. God wants the same from us.

But too often we focus on the part of Psalm 37:4 that says, "He will give you the desires of your heart" and leave out the conditions of that promise.

1. Be happy in God.
2. Give your life to God.
3. Trust God.

When we come to the place that we can do those things (and do them over and over again each day), we will discover over and over the desires of our heart.

Many, many years ago I surrendered my life to Christ. I sat in His presence and said, "I have no idea what I want to do with my life. What do you think I need?" I knew I could confidently ask Him that question and trust Him with the outcome because:

- God's the expert. "Behold, I am the Lord, the God of all flesh. Is anything too hard for me?" (Jer 32:27)
- God knows me and my heart. "For You formed my inward parts; You wove me in my mother's womb." (Ps 139:13)
- God loves me. "God shows his love for us in that while we were still sinners, Christ died for us." (Rom 5:8)
- God wants what's best for me. "For I know the plans I have for you," declares the LORD, "plans to prosper you and not to harm you, plans to give you hope and a future." (Jer 29:11)

And I've always loved my life!

Loving my life doesn't mean that I haven't had a lot of heartache, disappointment, and grief along the way. What it does mean is that my life is in the hands of the One who created me and died for me so that I could be redeemed. I live as the blood-bought daughter of The King, now and for all eternity! What's not to love about that?

"Delight yourself in the lord; and he will give you the desires of your heart. Commit your way to the Lord, trust also in him, and he will do it." (Ps 37:4-5)

All that I am or ever hope to be I owe to the power of the Holy Spirit at work in my life. As I look at my life, I see dreams and miracles in living color. I intend to celebrate the gift of this one life and honor my Lord and Savior by living and serving faithfully wherever He leads me.

May I ask you a question?

> What might God do through your life in the power of the Holy Spirit, if you were willing to dream big and believe in miracles? What might he accomplish through you if you would only throw off your cloak of worry and just enjoy the beauty, dance with the invisible music, and celebrate life?[1]

Dreaming big and believing in miracles doesn't mean we'll get everything we want in this life. In the fifth grade, momma was still calling the shots with my hairstyle and doing a great job. In the sixth grade, I wanted hair like Dorothy Hamill. In the eighth grade, I wanted hair like Farah Fawcett. In the tenth grade, I wanted hair like Blair from the TV show, *Facts of Life*.

Problem was, I wasn't them and I didn't have their hair. Before my expert hairstylist, a.k.a. my sister, I had willing hairdressers who did their best to satisfy the hairstyle dreams of a young girl. But those dreams never really worked and often looked like a mess instead of a miracle.

Give God your life. Admit to Him that you don't have a clue what to do with it. Ask Him what He thinks you need. Then sit back and trust Him with the outcome. I promise it will be beautiful because He's the expert in your life, He knows you and your heart, He loves you, and He wants what's best for you.

P.S. In case you're feeling like you've really messed up and it's too late for you, know this:

Bad haircuts and DIY color are no challenge for an expert. Just get yourself to a good salon and let them work their magic.

Bad choices and DIY life plans are no challenge for God either. Wherever you are, no matter how long you've been there, go to God and surrender your life. He's waiting for you.

Takeaway Truth

"Commit your way to the Lord; trust in him, and he will act." (Ps 37:5)

35

When You've Been Disappointed by Life

I'm a recovering, first-born, type-A, overachieving, perfectionistic, people-pleaser in desperate need of Jesus. I tend to see the glass "half-full". I'm always-looking-on-the-bright-side.

As a child I was full of hope and optimism and adventure. I thought anything was possible and I lived like it. But one who loved me very much, in an effort to guard my heart, often said, "I hate to see you get your hopes up because you might be disappointed."

Now I understand it was born out of her unspoken disappointments in life and her need to protect my tender heart but I couldn't conceive of ever being disappointed. So I continued to live full of hope and optimism.

Then life happened and the stuff that comes with life—there were a lot of little things and a few really, really big ones. I soon found myself disillusioned and disappointed. I started playing it safe and put my spirit of adventure, along with my heart, in a safe place on the shelf. I lived that way for a while.

I wasn't hopeless. I just lived with less hope.

But the Lover of My Soul, Jesus, spoke truth into my heart in the way that only He can. He showed me that my hope had been misplaced. Misappropriated.

Jesus helped me see:

- Hope in a man or a woman might lead to disappointment.
- Hope in a career or job might lead to disappointment.

• Hope in a church or a ministry might lead to disappointment.
• Hope in some achievement or success might lead to disappointment.
• Hope that life will turn out exactly as you hoped or planned might lead to disappointment.

People and organizations and plans fail and often leave us disillusioned and disappointed. There's someone reading this today who's disappointed. You feel really hopeless or at the very least you're living with less hope because it feels safer. It's hard to see the bright side or the glass half full.

I'm here today to remind you: Jesus is our hope, our only real hope in this life. He is the bright side of every circumstance. He is the living water that satisfies and fills us whether our glass is half-full or half-empty. And can I just tell you. . . He never, ever disappoints.

So get your hopes up! Please get you your hopes up. The world needs the hope that we have in Christ. Put your hope in Jesus—all of it or whatever you have left after life happens. You'll never be disappointed in Him.

"May the God of hope fill you with all joy and peace in believing, so that by the power of the Holy Spirit you may abound in hope." (Rom 15:13)

"But I will hope continually and will praise you yet more and more. My mouth will tell of your righteous acts, of your deeds of salvation all the day, for their number is past my knowledge." (Ps 71: 14-15)

Will you dare to hope again?

What are your hopes for your life?

I'm not talking about wishful thinking. Our hope is rooted in the salvation of Christ and the fact that he is the fulfillment of all Old Testament promises. The biblical definition of hope is confident expectation—a firm assurance. The righteous that trust in God will be helped according to Psalm 28:7. They will not be confused, put to shame, or disappointed. They have this trustful hope in God, a general confidence in God's protection and help, and are free from fear and anxiety

So let me ask you again. What are your hopes for your life? Would you be willing to write it down? Don't edit. Don't second guess yourself. Only you will see your list and God already knows all about the desires of your heart. Keep adding to your list as you think of the hopes you have, especially ones you may have had for a long time. After you make this list I want you to give it to God. Find a place where you can be alone and talk to God out loud just like you would to a good friend. Tell Him what your hopes are. Of course, he already knows but like any good friend he loves hearing it from you. Be boldly honest about your hopes, the people and circumstances they involve. Then pray, "Father God, I'm giving these hopes to you. You are my only hope. I trust you with my life. I trust you with these hopes. I ask you to renew my thoughts and feelings so that I hope for the right things in the right way. In Jesus' name, Amen."

Takeaway Truth

"And now, O Lord, for what do I wait? My hope is in you." (Ps 39:7)

36

When You're Feeling Distracted

"Develop interest in life as you see it; in people, things, literature, music---the world is so rich, simply throbbing with rich treasures, beautiful souls and interesting people. Forget yourself."
Henry Miller

What will it take for you to pay attention?
"Pay attention to what?" you might ask.
To your life, dear.

The Inconvenient Interruption

The doorbell rings just as I'm taking the empty coffee cup to the kitchen sink. I set it on the coffee table between the measuring tape and vintage typewriter. They each have a story to tell.

I answer the door and say a cheery "Good morning" to the young repairman standing there in a uniform and knee pads, with gadgets and tools hanging from his belt. I have mixed feelings about seeing him and his brightly colored van sitting in my driveway.

"How are you? He smiles and asks politely.

"Hot," I think to myself but I hesitate. (I'm determined to break my habit of complaining.)

"Hot?" he answers for me.

"Well a little. But only after I started moving around folding and putting away laundry," I reply.

He steps inside the door and maneuvers around the box fan in the floor Eric had set up before he left for work. It's September in the Deep South, the high today is 97 degrees. He takes a look at the thermostat in the hallway and asks some questions. I relay what I'd overheard during the call for service this morning.

He needed to see more to diagnose the problem so I lead him out the front door and down the sidewalk to the back yard. I notice the vibrant green Boston fern. It seems to love the spot at the end of the sidewalk, where the trees protect it from too much summer sun.

We follow the stepping stones around the corner of the house and crunchy leaves under my feet hint that fall is around the corner even if I am wearing a sundress and Birkenstocks. We walk under the shady canopy of the maple tree whose leaves will soon be a brilliant fiery orange. "I love this tree," I think to myself.

I stop momentarily to warn him about the dogs in the back yard. His dark eyes widen but I reassure him that he's in no danger. Except perhaps of not getting any work done due to one big female German shepherd who thinks everyone through the gate is there to entertain her.

"The other repairman always plays with her," I add.

He chuckles and says, "That must be Steve."

I notice a large web with a small garden spider blocking the gate. Using a small stick, I gently remove the web and lay the stick in the grass, giving the tiny creature a chance to rebuild.

I slip through the gate as the big dog waits anxiously on the other side. He stands a few feet behind me and the safety of the chain-link fence. I walk across the ankle-high grass and more crunchy leaves trying to lure her away with a game of fetch. Too late. She's already spotted a new friend.

She rears up on the fence gate. He just stands there looking at her. I get her attention and she gallops my way full-speed. Her other favorite game is "catch me if you can". And I never can. She's fast and agile. The leash fools her into thinking we're leaving the yard. She comes over quickly and with a click, I'm tethered to a 75-pound shedding ball of energy. Now I'm hot.

He begins his assessment and I decide to walk the dog up the stairs to the deck while he works. She's hesitant, knowing it's usually off-limits but she follows my lead. I position the umbrellas to create a shady spot for us both to sit and wait. She's hot and restless so I release my hold and let her find a cooler spot against the house.

Condensation drips down the sides of my tall glass of ice water as sweat rolls down the back of my neck. There's a light, warm breeze blowing and I look up to notice the curling leaves of the 200-year-old Tulip Poplar at the edge of the yard. The dry weeks are taking their toll. I notice the spiders have been busy here, too. Dozens of strands, stretched between chairs and plants, dance and glisten in the early morning sun.

Suddenly I hear what must be hundreds of cicadas singing. They've been there all along but I've only just heard. There are birds, too, calling out to one another. Heavy equipment roars in the background, reminding me that the golf course is becoming a new housing development and my lovely, old and quiet neighborhood is still lovely, but not so quiet.

The repairman calls out from the yard below. He's found the problem. It's not what he'd originally thought. It will take longer to fix.

I call my sister to cancel our appointment. She's kind and understanding. We both mention the sadness of not seeing each other today. For years I've driven two hours one way not because she's the only hairdresser I know (even though she is the best one), but because it's an appointment sisters need to keep. I suspect I'm not the only woman who sits in her chair on a regular basis for more than just "color and a cut."

I've been outside for almost an hour now. I'm reminded of how much I love being outside even when it's hot. The sights, sounds, and smells always take me back to the summers of my childhood.

The repairman calls out again, telling me he's done and instructing me to turn the thermostat to "cool" again. I step back into the house and notice it's not as hot as it seemed this morning.

Perspective.

I see the empty cup still sitting on the coffee table. I pick it up and take it to the kitchen sink.

What will it take for you to pay attention? For me, it was an inconvenient interruption.

Takeaway Truth

"You make known to me the path of life; in your presence there is fullness of joy; at your right hand are pleasures forevermore." (Ps 16:11)

37

When You’re Missing Home

Home is more than just a house. Home is bigger than four walls and a roof. Home is an atmosphere, a feeling, a sense of belonging. And you can take home with you wherever you go and share it with others who need to experience what home offers. As the mother of several young adult children, I've learned to take a little bit of home to them, wherever they are. We've logged a lot of miles to visit, meet halfway, and vacation together with the little pieces of our heart that grew up and left the home where we live on a tree-lined street at the foothills of the Appalachian Mountains in northeast Alabama.

I've hauled furniture, pets, and pots of soup in an effort to make my people feel at home wherever they've landed. But recently I learned another lesson about home.

Panama City Beach Road Trip

We went to visit our youngest son in Panama City Beach, Florida where he’s interning at a Christian youth camp. We hadn't seen him since summer began and were really looking forward to spending some quality time with him during his week off.

I packed the home-made cookies and gift-card his sister wanted me to give him and the few things he asked me to bring from home. I looked forward to taking him out to eat and shopping and spending a little time at the beach. But our first few hours together had me in tears.

I Cried at Target

Once we were settled into our room we decided to make a trip to Target to get some things he needed. Of course, we ended up in Starbucks and found ourselves gathered around a small wobbly table in the corner. Eric had a tall, strong coffee, I had a Dragon drink, and Caleb had a mocha-frappe-dingo (or something like that).

We were tired from the long hours in the car and he was tired from no-sleep-at-youth-camp. (I don't miss those days.) But he started sharing a little bit of what God had done in the previous month. I say "a little bit" not because God only did "a little bit" but because it's really difficult to adequately explain to others all that God does over a period of weeks. In other words, you had to be there.

But he shared one story that obviously had a huge impact on him and others. It was the kind of story with twists and turns and dates and places and people and coincidences that makes you say, "Only GOD could do THAT!"

There we were, all teary-eyed in Target, wallowing in the overflow of what God had done in him and them.

And we were home. Not physically at home. But home in the spiritual on-earth-as-it-is-in-heaven sense.

We often talk about God being invisible but I saw Him clearly in the coffee shop that day. He was there in the midst of bathing-suit-clad shoppers who smelled like salt air and sunscreen. I heard Him whisper above speaker phone conversations, coffee blenders, and restless babies.

"I'm your home, child. And his, too."

I thought I was taking a little bit of home to my boy. Turns out he already had everything he needed.

Jesus Is Our Home

He's our Hiding Place, our Daily Bread, and the Light that guides our way. He's our Comforter, Counselor, and Compassionate Friend. He's our Healer. Our Redeemer. The King of our Heart. He's our home. Wherever we go, He's there with us.

I'm thankful for the time we spent with him and the stories he told. And I didn't cry all the time. I also shopped a little and ate lots of good food!

Takeaway Truth

"I wash my hands in innocence and go around your altar, O Lord, proclaiming thanksgiving aloud, and telling all your wondrous deeds. O Lord, I love the habitation of your house and the place where your glory dwells." (Ps 26:7-8)

38

When You Need a New Game Plan

I love God and I love the way He loves me. Sometimes He loves me big---you know that over-the-top, mind-blowing, part-the-Red Sea kind of way. But I'm especially fond of the ways He loves me small. Not that His love is small, but the way He often shows His love is so private and personal and I'm reminded again that in a world spinning one thousand miles per hour and growing by one hundred and forty people every minute, He sees *me.*

It's the whisper only my heart can hear.

His still, small love blindsides me every time. I almost feel dizzy as the world around me fades away. I want to stop the clock, catch my breath, and hold onto the moment.

My Story

We grew up just a few miles apart in the same small town but I never got to see him play football. Under Friday night lights, he suited up as a defensive end for the Choctaws while I cheered for the Chargers across the river. Even though we saw each other from time to time, we didn't start dating until after we graduated high school.

For thirty-five years we've enjoyed talking football (yes I understand the game) and watching football together. Today we enjoyed some football talk. I asked him about the positions he played back in the day and the various defensive plays used in football. I'm sure it seemed like a random question. But God had whispered to my heart and I was leaning in close to listen and learn.

The Whisper Only Your Heart Can Hear

During church this week, we sang the chorus, "Lord, I Need You". It's still one of my all-time favorites. But this line, "You are my one defense" grabbed my attention like never before.

I sang the words out loud.

God whispered.

Holy Spirit convicted.

I was blindsided by the awareness that the Lord is often not my one defense.

When I see a problem, the opponent, I run through all the potential plays in my mind. I overthink, wring my hands, beat my chest, growl, and grunt. I am determined to halt or at least hinder Problem's progress.

Like a skilled player confident in my ability to keep my opponent from getting the upper hand or scoring points, I take my position, execute my defensive play, and shift my position or stance when necessary.

And time after time, I'm beat. My Opponent outmaneuvers me. My plays are no match for what lines up against me, seeking to devour me.

My One Defense

Today, my friend Jesus reminded me that He is my one defense. He----not me. Yet I live and move as if I am my one defense. As if winning at life is all up to me.

In football, no winning team has just one defensive play. But in life, One is all you and I need. Jesus is our One Defense. He's with us, enabling us to play the position and live the life He's created us to live. Together we're a winning team.

Friend, he sees you, too. He loves you in big ways and small. No doubt you've got a million things on your checklist today and you're determined to get most of them done. I know the feeling well. But will you let these words be your little reminder that Jesus is Your One Defense? He's all you need.

1. Look for His love. In His Word, He says, "I have loved you with an everlasting love; therefore I have continued my faithfulness to you." (Jer 31:3) In a world where nothing lasts forever and everything has a "best used by" date, you can rest assured that your

Father loves you. Always has. Always will. And more importantly, He wants you to know Him and His love. Ask Him to help you see His love in your life today.

2. Let Him love you. You are not unlovable to Him. I know it's easy sometimes to feel unloved and unlovable but that's a lie from the Enemy. "But God shows his love for us in that while we were still sinners, Christ died for us." (Rom 5:8). He created you and made a way for you to be redeemed and reconciled to Him. He knew what He was getting when He chose you! Let Him love you. Being loved, knowing you are loved is a game changer!

Takeaway Truth

"The steadfast love of the Lord never ceases; his mercies never come to an end." (Lam 3:22)

39

When You Labor in Obscurity

I eat cereal before I go to bed, sort laundry, mop old linoleum, teach Algebra I to my last student, and read lots of books. I run a few miles each week so I can eat cinnamon rolls, get my somewhat-crooked-teeth cleaned twice a year, and take a picture of the sky almost every day. I stay up until midnight, wake up too early, and take power naps when I can. With all that excitement you'd think I'd have my own reality show. Alas, I labor in obscurity.

But God.

Today is grocery shopping day. It's not my favorite day of the week but, I follow my list and try to get in and out as quickly as possible. I am focused and methodical. Frozen foods. Produce. Bakery. Almost done. And then he rounds the corner. My divine appointment.

I smile his way as I mentally chart the quickest way to the register. Just a few more items and . . .

"You probably love grocery shopping don't you?"

I pause and look his way. "Uh no, actually I don't like it very much at all." I smile and take another step.

"My wife has cancer and now I have to do all the shopping," he says pleasantly and matter-of-factly.

The words hang in the cool air as this stranger and I stand face to face. He looks tired with his uncombed hair and paper-thin plaid shirt.

"Why is he telling me this?" I wonder. "Why is he telling *me* this?"

My cart overflows with pieces of next week's life. His is almost empty. He looks at me with wet blue eyes and I look away, over his shoulder, to see the condensation trickle down the glass. I don't want to do this. I don't want to be here. I swallow the lump in my throat.

But God works all things together for good. Nothing's wasted.

"I understand just a little bit of what you're going through," I reply. "My dad did the shopping for years while my mother was sick. She died a few years ago."

"How's your dad doing now?" the stranger asks.

"He died in May," I reply, trying not to show my grief.

"Oh, I'm really sorry to hear that."

I listen as he talks about cancer, fear, loneliness, and grandchildren. Then the nudge. My Ever-Present-Father-Friend whispers, "Ask him about Me."

I silently object. "Not here, Lord. Not now."

No use arguing.

When the stranger pauses for a moment I gently ask, "Do you know the Lord?"

He cups his weathered hand around his ear. "'Scuse me. What did you say?"

So I repeat it loud enough for the lady buying frozen corn to hear, too. "Do you know the Lord?"

His face brightens. "Oh, yes! I've known Him for a long time. He's the only reason me and my wife have been able to make it through all this."

He and I talk of death and happy reunions and this bittersweet life. He extends his hand, tells me his name and where he lives. I take his hand and give him my name, too.

"I'm sure I'll be seeing you here again," he says as he turns to go. "And I'm awfully sorry about your dad."

"It was really nice to meet you," I say, meaning it.

God shows up in my ordinary life. Yours, too, I suspect. Ain't it grand? This life with God. God with us. God *with* us. God with *us*.

He takes all the pain, every loss, piles of disappointment, and grocery day and makes this life into something quite extraordinary.

Takeaway Truth

"And we know that God causes everything to work together for the good of those who love God and are called according to his purpose for them." (Rom 8:28)

40

When Grief is Weird

I never peel a cantaloupe that I don't think of her. She's been gone a decade. Mawmaw. My mother's mother. I don't know exactly why peeling a large piece of fruit reminds me of her but I'm glad it does.

Grief is Weird

And by weird I mean mysterious. Grief is sometimes difficult to understand, explain, or identify. If you look up the definition of 'mysterious' you'll find that the opposite of ‘mysterious’ is 'straightforward'. Grief is mysterious---the opposite of straightforward---weird.

5 Reasons Grief is Weird

1. We don't know how to do it. We can learn how to read, make brownies, and drive a car. But there's not a definitive set of instructions on how to grieve. I won't grieve like you and you won't grieve like your best friend. And most of the time we're convinced we're doing it wrong.

2. Grief isn't a straight line of thoughts, feelings, and actions. We like step by step instructions that tell us to "do this, then this". Grief isn't that way. Our thoughts and feelings and experiences are all over the place. Overwhelming sadness, anger, peace, resentment, gratitude, depression, fear, and hope can hit us in waves over a period of weeks and months or even all in the same day.

3. Every loss is different. Grief is a response to a loss and since every loss is different because we relate to people and situations differently; our grief responses will be different, too. There seems to

be no muscle memory when it comes to grief. If I've learned anything about what to expect with grief it's this: lose the expectations. Your journey through grief will be different with each loss.

4. There's not a definite timeline. We want to know when it will end. When will it not hurt so much? When will I feel normal again? But we can't make an appointment to grieve. Grief blindsides us at the most inconvenient times and places.

5. Grief can't be rushed, fixed, or bypassed. Loss is painful. Grieving is healing. At least a healthy grief is healing. Any attempt to rush, fix, or bypass grief can wound us more and prolong the healing process. By the way, 'healing' doesn't mean 'getting over it'.

I Still Cry

I still cry sometimes when I think of those I've lost in this life. My mother, father, grandparents, mother- and father-in-law, and three babies are only a memory now. I can't hug or call or visit them anymore.

Some days I don't cry at all. Some days a single tear rolls down my face. Some days it's a good, ugly cry.

There's nothing wrong with me. And if you still cry over your loss, there's nothing wrong with you either.

In 1997 I completed my dissertation. The subject was grief. It was the culmination of years of coursework, research, and writing to fulfill the requirements for my doctoral degree. Mostly it was my attempt to deal with my own unresolved grief. I was certain I'd learned everything there was to know about the subject. I was wrong.

After all my years of research, writing, reading, and grieving here's what I know for sure:

We're never prepared for a loss. Never. Whether it's the loss of a person or a position, grief hits hard.

We *can* learn to weave the loss into the fabric of our lives. The loss doesn't define us but it does become part of who we are.

We can find a new normal and live again. Our life isn't over after a loss.

A mundane task like peeling a cantaloupe becomes sacred when I remember my grandmother and her love for Jesus. (She's the reason I read my Bible every day.)

I'm certain I was her favorite grandchild but if you ask each of my cousins they'd tell you they were her favorite because that's how she made you feel. Loved and special.

God longs to comfort you in your grief. No matter how long it's been He hasn't forgotten about you or your loss. He won't shame you or trivialize your pain. But He does want you to invite Him into your grief and receive His comfort and healing.

“Our loving Lord is not just present, but nearer than the thought can imagine - so near that a whisper can reach Him.” --Amy Carmichael

Takeaway Truth

“To all who mourn in Israel, he will give a crown of beauty for ashes, a joyous blessing instead of mourning, festive praise instead of despair.” (Isa 61:3 New Living Translation)

41

When You Long to be Remembered

Before I begin reading through a book in the Bible, I read the introductory information given in the pages before the first chapter. Knowing the background, date, and purpose of the book helps me better understand what I read and make personal application. The biographical information preceding the book of Obadiah provided a timely message for me recently.

About Obadiah

As a writer, I'm always fascinated by other writers. I enjoy knowing how they live, their writing process, and what inspires them. I'm especially intrigued by the Old and New Testament writers. What an assignment!

The Book of Obadiah is the shortest book in the Old Testament with only one chapter containing twenty-one verses. According to the introduction in my study Bible to the book of Obadiah, the author is known only as "Obadiah, Servant/Worshiper of Yahweh," followed by this statement:

No additional information is available about him.[1]

Wow!

We live in a world of status updates and clever profiles, where everyone wants their voice and their message to be heard. The stage and the spotlight go to the bizarre and beautiful, the loud and laughable, or the ones with deep pockets and wide egos.

Everyone from the well-known to the unknown wants to be noticed and liked and followed. Every day we rubber-neck our way through the internet and life, attempting to entertain ourselves, satisfy our boredom, and find out the latest news that will matter little---if at all---in eternity.

Lest you think I'm on some wordy high horse over here, I'll confess I've wasted a lot of time crafting sentences to accompany the perfect profile pic that make me seem smart, savvy, spiritual, or whatever it is I'm trying to be at the moment.

And then I read the introduction to Obadiah.

No additional information is available about him.

Chuck Swindoll says this about the Book of Obadiah:

> As a worshiper of Yahweh, Obadiah placed himself in a position of humility before the Lord; he embraced his lowly place before the almighty God.
>
> That God sent a man named “worshiper of Yahweh” to the people of Edom was no mistake. Edom had been found guilty of pride before the Lord (Obad 1:3). They had thought themselves greater than they actually were; great enough to mock, steal from, and even harm God’s chosen people. But the “Lord GOD,” a name Obadiah used to stress God’s sovereign power over the nations, will not stand idly by and let His people suffer forever (Obad 1:1). Through Obadiah, God reminded Edom of their poor treatment of His people (Obad 1:12–14) and promised redemption, not to the Edomites but to the people of Judah (Obad 1:17–18). The nation of Edom, which eventually disappeared into history, remains one of the prime examples of the truth found in Proverbs 16:18: “Pride goes before destruction and a haughty spirit before a fall.”[2]

The Edomites were troublemakers and we cheer loudly as we see God pronounce judgment on those who harmed His people. I identify as "God's people" and maybe you do, too. But in this Book written by humble Obadiah, I see myself looking too much like the Edomites. I have been found guilty of pride before the Lord.

God sent a man named Obadiah who was content to be known and remembered only as "worshiper of Yahweh" to a woman (me) who claims to be a worshiper of Yahweh yet wants to be known and remembered for so much more.

The question is this: *Could I be an Obadiah, content only to be known and remembered as "worshiper of Yahweh"?* These words aren't meant to be commentary on the internet or social media, although I find both equally useful and deplorable.

This is just me thinking out loud about a few things:

- How pride rears its ugly head in my life (and maybe yours, too).
- How pride harms the Body of Christ.
- How His Divine plan would have me reading a Book in the 21st century that was written in the 6th or 7th century B.C. because He's still working on me!
- How that Book, classified as the minor-est of the Old Testament Minor Prophets, would affect a major shift in my soul.
- How a man, willing to remain otherwise unknown, would obediently pen inspired words_that would today, divide my soul and spirit, joints and marrow; judging the thoughts and attitudes of my heart.

One day you and I will eventually disappear into history. May we choose today to place ourselves in a position of humility before the Lord; and embrace our lowly place before the almighty God.

Takeaway Truth

"He must increase, but I must decrease." (John 3:30)

42

When You Have to Pick a Side

I grew up in a small town---actually on the outskirts of a small town. By outskirts, I mean down Highway 58 which some still refer to as 'old 82' because 'new 82' is now the bypass. You get the picture?

I was always a little envious of friends who lived in a subdivision. I can't remember why but the neat rows of houses wouldn't have suited the wanderlust that led me into the woods around my house during my childhood. Sometimes I'd end up miles from home resting by a tree, thinking. Certainly wouldn't let my kids do that now.

My daddy was happy when the bypass was complete and the traffic decreased. Not me. I missed it, really. Once when a friend spent the night at my house she asked how I could sleep with all that noise. I didn't know what she was talking about. (She lived in a subdivision.) I think it was the first time I'd heard the hum of the tires on that worn out blacktop.

For most people traveling northwest from Montgomery, Highway 82 was the main thoroughfare to Tuscaloosa. And we all know what's in Tuscaloosa. Everything. At least that's how I looked at it back then. Within thirty miles of my home, there was fast food, a mall, a movie theater, and The Bear.

The local traffic was always humming but Saturdays in the fall brought a special treat with worshipers headed to their shrine. I was a little envious of that, too. I didn't attend a college football game until after I was married but I shared in the excitement. They dressed in their team colors from head to toe, traveled in lively groups of friends and family, and seemed like the happiest people in the world on that day.

But I was an Auburn fan.

Back in the day, Alabama held the bragging rights. When I asked my daddy why we were Auburn fans (as if it were some unchangeable genetic predisposition) he said, "I cheer for the underdog." So I did.

The Price of Peace

I'm miles from home now and I'm not an Auburn fan anymore. Haven't been an Auburn fan for years. I married an Alabama fan; we had children who grew up to be Alabama fans; and while there are many divided households in this state, that doesn't work for me.

The drama was real, people. I tried hanging on to my team for a while but I hate conflict, even the kind involving a silly football game. So I baled. Became a traitor. After three decades of being an Auburn fan, I officially announced that I was an Alabama fan. Gasp!

I wear the team colors and plan football Saturdays around game times. To my father, my defection was one of the worst moments in history. He threatened to write me out of the will.

As if.

He still loved me and I continued to buy him Auburn stuff for his birthday. But I need peace in my life with my people, and it came to the point that hanging on just wasn't worth it. My allegiance to the past, to a team, to a crowd, to a way of life all became like the noisy hum of tires on a blacktop highway. Once I heard it I couldn't unhear it. The price for peace seemed high as I quietly considered my defection and my pride blindsided me a few times. In the end, the need for peace won.

Football in the south is serious business. If you move to Alabama the first question you'll have to answer is not "Where you from?" but "Who you for?" Neutrality is not an option.

That's how it is with obedience, except there's much more at stake than bragging rights. We have our allegiances to habits, people, and ideas, many of which are a constant source of conflict in our lives. But we've grown so accustomed to the noise that we don't hear it anymore. It takes fresh eyes and ears and hearts to help us see and hear. And there's the rub. It almost feels easier not knowing, not hearing, and not feeling the conflict.

Ignorance is not bliss when it comes to walking in obedience with our Father God. He is the winning team. This isn't just about cheering and wearing the team colors but being in the game ourselves and winning at life. Still, the price for peace seems high. A lot is at stake. Usually, our pride plays first-string or we claim some sort of spew-worthy-lukewarm neutrality. The heart is deceitful and will unquestionably choose the losing, destructive ways of disobedience rather than submit to God's Plan.

The result of our choice? We get tackled and eat dirt rather than run the gap made for us by grace and forgiveness.

The peace and joy of the Lord---being in an obedient right relationship with Him--- is worth it. Once we've made the decision we wonder why it took so long.

You may not have an allegiance to a team or ever consider switching sides. No problem. But in life, there's only one plan, one play, and one winning way. God is pursuing you, recruiting you, inviting you to be a part of all He has to offer. It's the chance of a lifetime. One that's too good to refuse.

So. Who are *you* for?

Takeaway Truth

"Choose this day whom you will serve?" (Josh 24:15)

43

When You Have a World-Weary Spirit

Did you sleep well last night? I probably didn't. These days I'm too hot, too cold, going to the bathroom, getting a drink of water, and going to the bathroom again to sleep well. But the truth is I've never really been a fall-asleep-when-my-head-hits-the-pillow-and-not-wake-up-till-morning kind of girl.

But there have been many times in my life when not only did I not sleep well; I was too troubled to sleep at all. Things were happening around me and to me that caused me to lie wide awake, tossing and turning, until finally I'd just give up on sleep and get out of bed. I'd often do a load of laundry, eat, turn on the TV, clean up the kitchen, eat, read, or eat. My options included anything I could do (quietly) to distract my mind without waking those in blissful slumber.

I read something recently that speaks to those restless, sleepless early morning hours.

"Early on the first day of the week, while it was still dark, Mary Magdalene went to the tomb and saw that the stone had been removed from the entrance." (John 20:1 NIV)

Early

'Early' is an adjective defined as happening or done before the usual or expected time. I suspect Mary wasn't much different from the rest of us. She woke up early, still troubled by the events on Friday, a Saturday without her friend, Jesus, and the tasks of the day ahead. Maybe she hadn't slept at all that night. But early—before the usual or expected time, she started her day.

Early on the first day of the week

The first day of the week was Sunday but it was her Monday—the day after the Sabbath, Saturday. No doubt she had her week's list of things to do and places to go. Life around her did not stop—would not stop—in the wake of a Passover week and a cruel cross and her Savior dying.

Early on the first day of the week while it was still dark

Most likely it was sometime between the hours of 3:00 and 6:00 AM as she slipped quietly out the door. I can see her as she walked carefully through the quiet, empty streets. The dark, early-morning-heavy kind of hopelessness and helplessness was weighing down on her. She had questions without answers and a pounding heart marking time until the light of day.

Early on the first day of the week, while it was still dark, Mary Magdalene

She was one of six different Mary's mentioned in the New Testament. This is the seven-demon Mary mentioned in Luke. The reference to seven demons most likely signifies the severe suffering she experienced when afflicted by their presence. She was perhaps wild-eyed and disheveled and loud or maybe sullen and withdrawn when possessed and oppressed. But when Jesus saw her he only saw the person she could be and would be once she was set free by His healing touch. And set free she was. No one superseded Mary Magdalene in her utter devotion to the Savior-Healer. She was one of the last followers at the cross and at his burial.

Early on the first day of the week, while it was still dark, Mary Magdalene went to the tomb

She was the first at the tomb. She went because she couldn't live a day without being with Jesus. This cave-like burial plot was the last place she saw him. She had watched and wept as Joseph of Arimathea had prepared his body and placed it in the tomb on Friday evening.

She had started out early, in the dark that Sunday morning; but, by the time she reached the tomb the sun had risen.

Early on the first day of the week, while it was still dark, Mary Magdalene went to the tomb and she saw

She saw that the Son had risen. She saw the empty tomb. She saw the Savior-Healer. What a great honor to be the first to witness the most important event in world history and the pivotal truth of Christianity, namely the Resurrection of Jesus Christ. She was given the privilege of announcing the greatest good news ever proclaimed: "Tell them that their Lord who had died is alive forevermore."

Here's what I learned:

1. Get up early. Whatever the week's events or tasks ahead, my days are better when I get up early. By early, I simply mean a few minutes before everyone else. I know this is easier at different times and seasons of life but if it is within your power get up early, before everyone else. There is no solace in fifteen minutes of sleep compared to what awaits you. Get up.

2. Go to Jesus. Go directly to Jesus. Bring your wild-eyed, disheveled heart to him. Bring your world-weary withdrawn spirit and let him heal you again. Because you can't live a day without being with Jesus. Oh, friend, you may breathe and work and think and plan 24-7. But you cannot live---really live---a single day without being with Jesus. So get up early and go to the tomb. Cast you cares there. Bury them dead. Cling to the Savior Alive.

3. Give Him everything. Give him your day. There are a thousand possibilities for how you live it. Allow him to show you the best ones. Give him your life. You may know exactly how you want it to look or you may not have a clue what to do with it. Invite Him to show you a better life than you could ever imagine. Give him you. It's what He wants and He's what you need more than anything.

Get up early. Go to Jesus. Give him everything. What He'll give you in return is much better than a little extra sleep.

Takeaway Truth

"Let the morning bring me word of your unfailing love, for I have put my trust in you. Show me the way I should go, for to you I entrust my life." (Ps 143:8)

44

When You're Overthinking Everything

The human spirit is so weak that when it would look too curiously into the causes and reasons of God's will it embarrasses and entangles itself in the meshes of a thousand difficulties, out of which it has much to do to deliver itself; it resembles smoke, for as smoke ascends it gets more subtle, and as it grows more subtle it vanishes. In striving to raise our reasonings too high in divine things by curiosity we grow vain or empty in our thoughts, and instead of arriving at the knowledge of truth, we fall into the folly of our vanity.
--St. Francis de Sales

I'm an over-thinker. To be an over-thinker simply means you think about something too much for too long. Here's how good I am at overthinking: If overthinking were an Olympic sport, I'd have a gold medal. If someone would pay me for my overthinking skills, I'd be a millionaire. My husband says that I even overthink thinking.

Overthinking is not a spiritual gift and it's certainly not anything to brag about. It's actually a hindrance to walking by faith and living a Spirit-filled life.

Why? Because overthinking is usually an attempt to do the following:

1. Figure it out. Why did this happen? What might happen?
2. Fix, control, or manage a person or situation. What can I do about them/it? How can I prevent it from happening? How can I fix them/it?

As St. Francis de Sales wrote, we find ourselves "entangled in the meshes of a thousand difficulties" and "instead of arriving at the knowledge of the truth, we fall into the folly of our vanity."

This week I was waiting in the car at Walmart for my daughter and I was in full-blown over thinking mode. Thinking, thinking, thinking, trying to figure it all out and fix it. Very clearly I heard the Holy Spirit speak to my heart, "Overthink Joy."

Wow!

I decided to give it a try because I'm weary of the struggle with the tangled mess of my own thoughts. You know what I've learned? The more I think about joy and look for the joy in my circumstances the more I see and experience joy.

I'm not suggesting we live in a state of denial about all the things that are going on in our lives but there's so much we can't fix or manage or control no matter how much we overthink them.

We need to fight for joy and fight back with joy.

Here are three of my favorite verses that help me when I'm tempted to overthink:

1. "Therefore, since we are surrounded by such a great cloud of witnesses, let us throw off everything that hinders and the sin that so easily entangles. And let us run with perseverance the race marked out for us." (Heb 12:1 NIV)

I've come to see overthinking as a sin that entangles me.

2. "We destroy arguments and every lofty opinion raised against the knowledge of God, and take every thought captive to obey Christ," (2 Cor 10:5)

My overthinking is me setting my mind, my thoughts, against the knowledge of God.

3. "For as the heavens are higher than the earth, so are my ways higher than your ways and my thoughts than your thoughts." (Is 55:9)

I will never be able to power up over the thoughts and ways of God.

Overthinking is exhausting and futile. Our mind is an incredible gift from God and we have the power to choose what we think about!

Takeaway Truth

"Finally, brothers, whatever is true, whatever is honorable, whatever is just, whatever is pure, whatever is lovely, whatever is commendable, if there is any excellence, if there is anything worthy of praise, think about these things." (Phil 4:8)

45

When You Need the Gospel in the Middle of the Mess

When we moved into our house years ago we noticed a large crack in the ceiling near the attic stairs in the garage; but, it appeared the previous homeowners had repaired it. Unfortunately, their solution was little more than a Band-Aid on a gaping wound. Over the years the crack got larger and longer and soon the garage ceiling began to cave under a weight it was not built to bear.

We called a professional who diagnosed the problem. Sadly, it was worse than we'd thought. The original construction was all wrong and the ceiling would need to be torn out and rebuilt. It was a costly, messy project.

To make matters worse we would have to use some of the money we were saving for a kitchen project. My dream for a beautiful, more functional kitchen that our family and friends could enjoy had been hijacked. Our time and energy would now be focused on repairing the attic in the garage. I cried over this, people.

For weeks I tripped over the junk that came out of the attic and out of my heart. I pushed around and rearranged to make way for the builders and the construction project that took longer and cost more than expected. .

The Gospel in the Middle of My Mess

More important than new attic space, I gained a new perspective because my good, good Father never, ever misses an opportunity to teach me His ways.

One afternoon as I stood knee deep in my discouraged mess looking up at the newly completed construction project (that no one will ever see but me) God did what He does so well. He took my face in His kind and gentle hands and showed me the bigger picture.

He is constructing my life and sometimes that requires tearing out what's not fit to house a King and bear the weight of His glory.

So much of the deconstruction and remodeling He does in us through the years is costly and messy. As the Master builder He works in the heart and mind, changing our perspective, our attitudes, and our thinking. He doesn't waste time with quick fixes or cosmetic updates. He is less concerned with our outward beauty and more concerned with our heart. Band-Aids will not do.

And so He tears away the parts of our life that have been poorly constructed by our own unskilled hands and in return gives us a happy hiding place in Him and the good hope of heaven as our eternal dwelling place.

What more could we long for?

Takeaway Truth

"For we know that if the tent that is our earthly home is destroyed, we have a building from God, a house not made with hands, eternal in the heavens. For in this tent we groan, longing to put on our heavenly dwelling," (2 Cor 5:1-2)

46

When You Feel Alone

I am with you always.

These were the final Gospel words of Jesus to his disciples---and to us. How did he know? How did he know we would so desperately need His presence with us always? Of all the promises He could make to us, why this one?

Why not promise "I'll make you successful".

Why not promise "I'll make you happy".

Why not promise "I'll make it easy".

But He knew what we didn't know….

"And about the ninth hour Jesus cried out with a loud voice, saying, 'Eli, Eli, lema sabachthani?' **that is,** "My God, my God, why have you forsaken me?" (Matt 27: 46)

The last two words in this cry of our Savior on the cross are Aramaic (the everyday language spoken by Jesus).

In some sense Jesus had to be cut off from the favor and fellowship with the Father that had been his eternally, because he was bearing the sins of his people and therefore enduring God's wrath.[1]

He experienced God-forsakenness **so that we would never have to know life without Him.**

He knew His presence was everything. He is El Shaddai, the All-Sufficient One. So that's the promise He made. I am with you always.

In one of my favorite spiritual classics, *Practicing His Presence*, Brother Lawrence wrote:

> We need to recognize that God is intimately present with us and address Him every moment. In things that are doubtful

we need to ask His assistance to know His will. And the things we plainly see He requires of us, we should rightly perform. As we go about this pursuit we should simply offer all things to Him before we do them and give Him thanks when we have finished.

What are you facing today? What need do you have? As a believer in Jesus Christ, **you are not alone**. The Lord is not outside of you, pouring down favors. **The Lord is within you**. Seek Him there, within, . . . and nowhere else.[2]

Takeaway Truth

"For I am sure that neither death nor life, nor angels nor rulers, nor things present nor things to come, nor powers, nor height nor depth, nor anything else in all creation, will be able to separate us from the love of God in Christ Jesus our Lord." (Rom 8:38-39)

47

When You're Too Focused on Success and Failure

We sing songs of praise, my family and me on that bright Sunday morning. The sanctuary feels like home. I am happy to be here, surrounded by my children who stand a head taller than me and are growing in a faith they've made their own.

I look around the room at all the familiar faces and that's when I catch of glimpse of her, a church friend who criticizes and shines the brightest of lights on every mistake I make. She questions my motives. The weight of my failure sits heavy and I realize I have stopped singing. Stopped smiling. The lump in my throat and the knot in my stomach are a familiar feeling this recovering people-pleaser had almost forgotten.

Soon my eyes see a friendly face. She always promises intercession and delivers well. She speaks encouragement and highest praise. I feel the lump in my throat and knot in my stomach again.

My potential to fail and disappoint both critic and champion sits heavy. Criticism and praise. Criticism and praise. Criticism and praise. I fall headlong into the extremes.

Criticism and praise can be dangerous weapons in the hands of our Enemy. He uses both in an attempt to destroy us.

Have you known criticism and praise? I know you have. This is the stuff of a thousand "church stories" but the experience isn't confined to the meeting place of the Body of Christ. The Enemy prowls around in all the places we live and work and play. The cycle of criticism and praise rolls through your workplace, your home, and the ballpark. The silent dread of family reunions, lunch meetings, and school functions creates a knot in your stomach that cannot be untangled. At the end of the day, you crawl into bed exhausted from the roller coaster ride of criticism and praise, criticism and praise, criticism and praise.

I know how to beat the Enemy at his own game.

1. Repeat after me: "He rejoices over me with singing." Seriously. Repeat after me. Did you say it? Whisper it if you must but please say it. Truth annihilates the lie that The Accuser uses to infect and kill and destroy you.

Father God rejoices over you and me with singing. He tells us so in Zephaniah 3:17. He reminds us how God feels about His children. He knows all that we've said and done and the motives of our heart. He created us and pursues us with unfailing love. He is not surprised or disillusioned by you and me. He rejoices over us with singing. Because He sees past all that we are to the One who lives inside us.

2. Repeat after me: "The only thing that's good in me is Jesus." The words are a deadly poison to your Enemy and medicine to your soul. When the Enemy uses someone to remind you of all your failures, agree with him. He's right. The Apostle Paul knew the struggle was real.

“So I find this law at work: Although I want to do good, evil is right there with me. For in my inner being I delight in God’s law; but I see another law at work in me, waging war against the law of my mind and making me a prisoner of the law of sin at work within me. What a wretched man I am! Who will rescue me from this body that is subject to death? Thanks be to God, who delivers me through Jesus Christ our Lord!” (Rom 7:21-25 NIV)

And when the Enemy uses someone to pour out praise that threatens to puff up your pride, accept that praise for the sake of Christ. Paul knew about that, too.

“But by His doing you are in Christ Jesus, who became to us wisdom from God, and righteousness and sanctification, and redemption, so that, just as it is written, ‘LET HIM WHO BOASTS, BOAST IN THE LORD.’" (I Cor 1:30-31 New American Standard Bible)

There will always be those who have heard (or know as fact) something you've said or done and they think less of you for it. And there will always be those who have heard (or know as fact) something you've said or done and they think too highly of you for it.

When you tear it all away---the criticism-worthy mistakes and the praiseworthy accomplishments---the only thing that's good in you and me is Jesus.

Our Enemy is relentless in his desire to see us throw in the towel. He'll do anything to make us forget who we are and whose we are. Beat him at his own game. Untie the knots he's using to bind you. Remind him that you've been set free and watch him run! The Thief is always thieving, but Jesus has come to give us life!

Takeaway Truth

"And the testimony is this that God has given us eternal life, and this life is in His Son." (I John 5:11)

48

When You Don't Know What to Pray

I'm a big fan of professional counselors and not just because I'm married to one. Many of the ones I've known have been dear friends and I know first-hand their passion for helping people. They bless others every day with their gift of listening and understanding. I've also heard the grateful testimony of individuals who have been helped by a counselor. Sometimes, however, you have a pain too deep for words.

The Groanings of My Heart

Life has difficult seasons. I lie in bed thinking about the storms I've survived and run through a list in my head: The death of my mother and father; a difficult season in our marriage; the joys and challenges of parenting; menopause; disappointment at church; and family conflict.

These issues, along with several others I didn't mention, give me a score of over 300 on *The Holmes and Rahe Stress Inventory*. According to their scoring interpretation, I have "a high or very high risk of becoming ill in the near future." That's the impact of long-term stress.

Maybe I need a counselor. I need to pour out my heart to someone who will understand without judging. I need to cry with someone who is familiar with tears and comfortable with silence. I need to confide in someone who can remove the shame and guilt I feel over past mistakes. I need a strong-someone who can lift the ten-ton elephant sitting on my chest. And I need that someone on speed dial, 24-7.

My life is rich with godly friends and family who know me and love me. They've spent hours listening over coffee, reading long emails and texts, or holding on to the phone as I rant. I am so very thankful for their faithfulness and wouldn't want to do life without them. In addition, several godly, professional counselors are within a short drive of my home.

But sometimes my heart is two-weeks-overdue with thoughts and feelings and hurt and disappointment that even I can't put into words or on a list. Sometimes, in spite of being surrounded by faithful friends and family and counselors, I have a heart loneliness that feels almost unbearable.

If I've said it once, I've said it a hundred times. "I just wish I had someone to talk to who really knew what my heart is feeling." I didn't say it out loud the morning I made my mental list but I thought it. And the One who always knows what my heart is feeling, the One and Only One who truly knows me, spoke to me these five words: "groanings too deep for words."

I knew what He was talking about. I knew He was telling me to go to the Source of Truth and Comfort—The Word. I read His inspired words from Romans 8:26-27 in The Message:

> Meanwhile, the moment we get tired in the waiting, God's Spirit is right alongside helping us along. If we don't know how or what to pray, it doesn't matter. He does our praying in and for us, making prayer out of our wordless sighs, our aching groans. He knows us far better than we know ourselves, knows our pregnant condition, and keeps us present before God. That's why we can be so sure that every detail in our lives of love for God is worked into something good.

And here's the same passage in the English Standard Version,

> Likewise the Spirit helps us in our weakness. For we do not know what to pray for as we ought, but the Spirit himself intercedes for us with groanings too deep for words. And he who searches hearts knows what is the mind of the Spirit, because the Spirit intercedes for the saints according to the will of God.

Life has its seasons. Some of them are really long and hard. Most of us are blessed with the dearest kind of friends who are faithful during those times. Sometimes we even make an appointment with a good counselor. But even then there are wordless sighs and aching groans that they cannot know. But oh praise God there is One who knows, a counselor—The Counselor—who knows my heart and understands.

He is familiar with tears and comfortable with silence. With Him, I feel no shame or guilt. He is the One who can help me bear the heaviest weight in my life. I need that counselor. How about you?

I am so thankful for the ever-present Holy Spirit in my life that perfectly comforts, guides, convicts, and encourages. Have you spoken to The Counselor today? He is ready and waiting to hear from you.

Takeaway Truth

"And I will ask the Father, and he will give you another Helper, to be with you forever, even the Spirit of truth, whom the world cannot receive, because it neither sees him nor knows him. You know him, for he dwells with you and will be in you. I will not leave you as orphans; I will come to you." (John 14:16-18)

49

When You Wake Up Tired

It's Sunday morning and I'm tired. I have a headache and my toothache reminds me of the major dental work happening in the morning. "Maybe I should just stay home and rest," I say to myself. Eric and I lie still and quiet as we watch the early morning sun dance on the walls around the room.

"What are you thinking about?" he asks.

"I'm thinking about staying home today," I answer. I hardly finish the sentence before tears well up in my tired, sleepy eyes. "But God has been so good to me. This week was hard and God was with me just like He promised." I am reminded again that my Savior's presence is everything.

Eric reaches over and gently wipes a tear off my cheek

"On Sunday, I go to church. It's a lifelong habit that has served me well. My parents and grandparents instilled it in me and modeled faithfulness week after week, year after year. In fifty-four years, I've missed very few Sundays at church." I repeat this fact as if he doesn't already know.

And then we do what we've always done on Sunday morning, without discussion. He makes coffee and we get dressed and go to church.

We're living in super weird times and even church feels weird. I miss the way it used to be. The distance between us is loud and the music is louder than I'd prefer at times. I don't always know the songs we sing and have trouble singing the ones I know. But the kindness of God washes over me and I feel His presence once again. So I sing and lift holy hands, grateful to be redeemed.

I notice the man sitting six feet over. He's frail and fidgety. "Juicy Couture" is big and bold on the back of his t-shirt tucked neatly into faded, oversized pajama pants. He doesn't know any of the songs but he taps his old tennis shoe to the beat. During the sermon, he sleeps.

I look around and marvel at all the different people in the same room. What in the world?

My head hurts and it's cold in here. I take another sip of my water trying to rehydrate after getting too hot yesterday. My tooth throbs and I think of my dental procedure tomorrow. Fear creeps in. I remember all the unresolved issues from last week.

And then a man called by God reminds me—us—of the difference between the Kingdom of Heaven (where God rules and reigns) and the Kingdom of the World (where sin reigns). I take three pages of notes because I know I'll need a reminder next week.

The Kingdom of Heaven is where I want to be. Love rules and reigns with absolute authority. But I live in a frail, fallen kingdom. I'm discouraged and tired. I need some Good News.

At the end, he says, "We live in the fallen Kingdom of the World but through Christ, we have the Kingdom of Heaven in our heart."[1]

Yes! I feel it.

"But we have this treasure in jars of clay to show that this all-surpassing power is from God and not from us. We are hard pressed on every side, but not crushed; perplexed, but not in despair; persecuted, but not abandoned; struck down, but not destroyed. We always carry around in our body the death of Jesus, so that the life of Jesus may also be revealed in our body. For we who are alive are always being given over to death for Jesus' sake, so that his life may also be revealed in our mortal body." (2 Cor 4:7-11)

The Gospel fills my heart with hope again.

A young woman comes forward to share her decision to follow Christ. She said she's grown up in church—-her dad was a pastor—-but now head knowledge has become heart transformation. I look around again and see all the different people, clapping and smiling and celebrating. And for a moment, I get a glimpse of The Kingdom of Heaven. I see it with my own two eyes.

The service has ended and I round up my things and make my way to the car. I notice a young woman crying. "Are you okay?"

"No, not really," she whispers.

We sit down in a quiet place and she tells me, in one sentence, her heartbreak. For a moment, I forget about social distancing and touch her arms crossed protectively on her chest.

"I'm so sorry," I reply.

She wipes away a tear and we sit quietly in His presence.

The Kingdom of Heaven is at hand. Both John the Baptist and Jesus said so. Today I felt it, saw it, and touched it.

"You glad we went to church today?" Eric asks as we're driving home.

I just look at him and smile.

Takeaway Truth

"I love your sanctuary, LORD, the place where your glorious presence dwells." (Ps 26:8 NLT)

50

When You Want to Do More Than Just Survive

"The Lord will not wish to count my trophies, but my scars."
Frank Laubach

Have you wavered in abiding? Jesus invited us, commanded even, to abide in Him "so that we would bear much fruit". (John 15:4)

Abide: to remain stable or fixed; to continue in a place; to accept without objection; to hang around with.

Bear: have or display a visible mark or feature; display, exhibit, show.

We work hard to bear fruit, or so we think, but in truth, we're working hard to produce fruit. We're makers, achievers, and ladder-climbers building our towers to the sky; trophies to our effort and ingenuity.

Our highest calling is to abide in Christ. He is the Vine that produces the fruit. We are simply to bear (display/exhibit/show) that which He produces (brings into existence/constructs/builds).

Have you wavered in abiding? Have you come to abide in other things? One way to know if you've wavered in abiding is this: have you lost your peace? I'm not asking if your world or your life is peaceful. I'm asking if you've lost your peace.

"For He, Himself is our peace," (Eph 2:14)

Jesus is our peace. If we're abiding in him, the world around us can be chaotic and dysfunctional, and we will have peace within because Jesus is our peace. Abiding brings peace.

Are You Abiding or Just Surviving?

"And a highway shall be there, and it shall be called the Way of Holiness; the unclean shall not pass over it. It shall belong to those who walk on the way; even if they are fools, they shall not go astray. No lion shall be there, nor shall any ravenous beast come up on it; they shall not be found there, but the redeemed shall walk there. And the ransomed of the Lord shall return and come to Zion with singing; everlasting joy shall be upon their heads; they shall obtain gladness and joy, and sorrow and sighing shall flee away." (Isa 35:8-10)

Have you veered off the Highway of Holiness and onto the pathway of your own thoughts and plans, acting as if Jesus were absent? Have you come to abide in social media, reading and watching the opinions of others, humored by one and frustrated by another? Have you come to abide in TV, Netflix, Amazon Prime, and your favorite news outlet? Are your hours spent glued to what our grandparents wisely referred to as "the idiot box"? Oh, but you know how to go through the motions of daily Bible reading, devotional reading, and church attendance. You are moved, convicted, and inspired. But have you wavered in abiding---practicing the presence of Christ---moment by moment? Would you be willing to commit or recommit to abiding---what Frank Laubach referred to as "filling every minute full of the thought of God"?

He says this in his classic book, *Practicing His Presence*:

> You will object to this intense retrospection. Do not try it unless you feel dissatisfied with your own relationship with the Lord, but at least allow me to realize all the leading of God I can. Paul speaks of our liberty in Christ. I am trying to be utterly free from everybody, free from my own self, but completely enslaved to the will of God every moment of this day.[1]

Practicing the presence of God in every hour and many times throughout the day will change your life. Jesus is with us, just as He promised, but everything changes when we become aware of His presence.

You might speak and act differently if your pastor or parent is present to hear and see you. Consider now that Jesus *is* present with you and He not only hears what you say and sees your actions, but He knows every thought.

We sing "All to Jesus I surrender, All to Him I freely give, I will ever love and trust Him, In His presence daily live." In His presence daily live. Abiding.

His presence is a comfort to us in times of distress and grief. Why should it not comfort us every moment of every day? Think of how it might change you.

I suppose the question is this: Do we want to be changed? We want the world---the people around us, the ones who lead and govern us---to change. But do we want to be changed? Do we really want to walk the Highway of Holiness? Do we want what the prophet Isaiah said belongs to the redeemed?

- everlasting joy upon our heads
- gladness and joy
- sorrow and sighing fleeing away

Peace. We cannot walk there without Him.

Takeaway Truth

"Abide in Me, and I in you. As the branch cannot bear fruit of itself unless it abides in the vine, so neither can you unless you abide in Me. I am the vine, you are the branches; he who abides in Me and I in him, he bears much fruit, for apart from Me you can do nothing." (John 15:4-5)

Conclusion

"Trust in him at all times, O people; pour out your heart before him; God is a refuge for us." (Ps 62:8)

The chorus of an old gospel song I learned in the little country church where I grew up has come to mind in recent days:

Where could I go, O where could I go
Seeking the refuge for my soul?
Needing a friend, to save me in the end
Where could I go but to the Lord?[1]

When life is hard I pray you'll turn to these reminders again and again and be encouraged to lean on God. You won't have to look far to find Him. He's in all the hard places waiting to lovingly comfort and guide you.

He was in the pit with Joseph, the jail cell with Paul, and the lion's den with Daniel. He was on the mountain of sacrifice with Abraham and Isaac, in the wilderness with David, and in captivity with the exiles. And He is with you wherever you are.

When life is hard, God is near. In Him you'll find everything you need.

Notes

Chapter 3

1. Oswald Chambers, *My Utmost for His Highest* (New Jersey: Barbour and Company, Inc., 1963), 54.

Chapter 4

1. Sam Middlebrook, *Introduction to Habakkuk in the Spirit-Filled Life Bible* (Nashville: Thomas Nelson, Inc., 1991), 1339.

Chapter 7

1. Bill Hybels, *Too Busy Not to Pray: Slowing down to be with God* (Illinois: Intervarsity Press, 1988), 13.

Chapter 9

1. *Under the Tuscan Sun,* directed by Audrey Wells, (Touchstone Pictures, 2003).

Chapter 13

1. *"Isaiah 6," Bible Hub, Matthew Henry's Commentary,* accessed November 18, 2020, https://biblehub.com/commentaries/mhc/isaiah/6.htm.
2. Ibid.
3. Gary Moreland, *Scary Hope: Courage and a kick to hug hope, face fear, and get going* (North Carolina, 2012), 137-144, Kindle.

Chapter 14

1. Mark Buchanan, *The Rest of God: Restoring your soul by restoring Sabbath* (Nashville: Thomas Nelson, 2006), 50.

Chapter 18

1. Russell Helms, *60 Hikes with 60 Miles: Birmingham* (Birmingham, Menasha Ridge Press, 2008), 59.

Chapter 25

1. Oswald Chambers, *My Utmost for His Highest* (New Jersey: Barbour and Company, Inc., 1963), 193.

2. C.S. Lewis, *Mere Christianity* (San Francisco: Harper One, 1943).

Chapter 32

1. Haley DeMarco and Michael DiMarco, *Die Young: Burying yourself in Christ* (Wheaton, IL: Crossway, 2012), 105.

2. Aimee Joseph, *"Enough with 'I am enough,'"* last modified February 15, 2018, http://thegospelcoalition.org/article/biblical-non-negotiables-origins-universe/.

Chapter 33

1. Sally Clarkson, *Own Your Life: Living with deep Intention, bold faith, and generous love* (Carol Stream, IL: Tyndale Momentum, 2015), 86.

Chapter 34

1. Clarkson, *Own Your Life,* 72.

Chapter 41

1. Timothy Mark Powell, *Introduction to Obadiah in the Spirit-Filled Life Bible* (Nashville: Thomas Nelson, Inc., 1991), 1302.

2. Chuck Swindoll, *Obadiah,* last modified November 24, 2020, https://www.insight.org/resources/bible/the-minor-prophets/obadiah.

Chapter 46

1. Michael J. Watkins, *study note on Matthew 27:46 in the ESV Study Bible* (Wheaton, IL: Crossway, 2008), 1886.

2. Brother Lawrence and Frank Laubach, *Practicing His Presence* (Sargent, GA: SeedSowers, 1973), 55.

Chapter 49

1. W. Mack Amis, *"Kingdom Living in a Fallen World",* Sermon, Parker Memorial Baptist Church, Anniston, AL, August 29, 2020.

Chapter 50

1. Lawrence, *Practicing His Presence,* 3.

Conclusion

1. James B. Coats, *"Where Could I Go"* (Stamps Baxter Recording and Printing Co, 1940).

Made in the USA
Columbia, SC
01 May 2025

57337435R00107